DEDICATION & ACKNOWLEDGMENTS

For Zoe and Tess.

I'd like to thank my husband, David Lincecum, for your encouragement and support. Melissa Matthay and Jeanne Leep, my dear friends who showed me the way to do this and told me I could. The lovely and patient Joy Aquilino, for believing in this project from the day we met, and to John Foster, Jess Morphew, Kara Plikaitis, and Autumn Kindelspire at Watson-Guptill. To my dear friend and agent Lucy Childs at Aaron Priest Literary Agency, thank you for being my guide on this new adventure.

Thank you to photographers Michael Turek and Timothy Hughes, for your extraordinary images. To Hannah Murray, Ken Udell, and Nicole White for your beautiful work. To Amy Butler and Linda Sandin at Amy Butler Designs; Westminster Fibers; Oilcloth International; Brian Kress and Fiskars; Laura Lambaseder and everyone at Nancy's Notions; Scott Holme at Carsey Werner; Kristin Johnston, Bridget Fonda, Gloria Tacchino, Carol Caplon, and Leah Sandholm, thank you for your generous support.

Many thanks to Melina Root, Lori Eskowitz-Carter, Mark Bridges, Louise Mingenbach, Isis Mussenden, Ruth Myers, Ann Roth, Aggie Guerard Rodgers, Ainslie Bruneau, Judith Dolan, David Woolard, the late Richard Hornung, and Motion Picture Costumers Local 705, especially Ernesto Martinez, Henry Po, Ellen Allen, Madline Hana, Pablo Nantas, Sherrie Mardirosian, Terri Lewis, Johnny Foam, Michelle Kurpaska, Mynka Draper, Lori Sacks, Tommy Marquez, Julia Bartholomew, Lisa Wilson, Therese McDonough, Craig Ames, and Andrea Federman. I'd also like to express my sincere gratitude for all the people who've inspired me on my path, especially my teachers and advisors Phil Atlakson, Mary Anne Hempe, Yslan Hicks, Kij Greenwood, Rich Corzatt, and Ludmilla Adams.

To my tribe, Ashley Lerblance, Teresa Compton, Donna Price, Ezma Schoemann, and Dora Schoemann, who taught me to be creative and resourceful.

To my precious friends Marn Turley, Stevie Corzatt, Etta Smith, Laurie Macgillivray, Marit Sathrum, Lisa Tresch, Andrew Naugher, Kay Windowski, and the Women Seeking Serenity, thanks for your kindness and curiosity.

CONTENTS

5   Acknowledgments
8   Preface

CHAPTER 1:
The Basics

14   The Rub-Off: Two Methods
16   Tools and Equipment
20   Fabric
22   Estimating Yardage
23   Taking Measurements
24   Sewing Essentials

CHAPTER 2:
Patterning Skirts

28   The Source Skirt
29   The Paper Rub-Off Method
47   Skirt Variations
49   Casual Denim Skirt
50   Wool Tweed Pencil Skirt
54   Striped A-Line Skirt
57   Reversible Cotton Wrap Skirt
60   Cotton Bias-Cut Skirt

CHAPTER 3:
Patterning Dresses

66   The Source Dress
67   The Fabric Rub-Off Method
85   Dress Variations
86   Retro V-Neck Dress
90   A-Line Money Dress
92   Inner Audrey Princess Seam Dress
94   Vintage Shop 'Til You Drop Dress
96   Pin-Up Halter Dress

CHAPTER 4:
Patterning Blouses

102   The Source Blouse
125   Blouse Variations
126   Green Apple Blouse with Cuffs
128   Little Black Blouse with Darts
130   Cap Sleeve Summer Sky Blouse
132   Rock-a-billy Halter Top
134   Shanti Tunic

CHAPTER 5:
Patterning Handbags

140 The Source Handbag
149 Handbag Variations
150 Bamboo Handbag
152 5 O'Clock Handbag
154 Ladylike Tote
156 Yoga Bag
160 Fur Clutch

164 Resources
166 Glossary
172 Index
176 Metric Conversion Chart

PREFACE

Today, we live in such abundance that anything we need can be purchased, not just at the local store, but with a single click on the computer (in our pajamas, no less) and delivery guaranteed for the next day. This is a wonderful thing—except that we've forgotten how to make things for ourselves. The conveniences of modern living have all but eliminated the empowerment and joy that comes from making something with what we have on hand. Creative skills that were once handed down from generation to generation were lost, seen for a time as dowdy and obsolete. Thankfully that's changing.

When I was a little girl I spent hours making clothes and elaborate furnishings for my Barbies. As was the case for so many kids of my generation, washcloths, Kleenex, and shoeboxes were my medium. I also remember spending many a long afternoon, playing contentedly under the quilting frame in my babysitter's spare bedroom, watching her as she zigzagged a needle through layers of backing, batting, and hand-pieced quilt tops.

In college, I found a use for my sewing skills in the theatre department's costume shop. I hadn't learned about "draping" or "flat patterning" yet, and didn't own a dress form, but when I couldn't find the right pattern I would intuitively make my own from existing garments. Later, a summer job as a stitcher at the Oklahoma Shakespeare Festival taught me many tricks of the trade. From the costume designer, I learned how to blow up 1/8-inch scale patterns from reference books and how to drape muslin to create patterns from scratch. I knew immediately that this is what I wanted to do as my career.

After earning my MFA in costume design I began a theater internship at the George Street Playhouse in New Jersey. While researching and pulling a few vintage pieces for a show at a costume rental house in Manhattan, I noticed a beautiful tweed Norfolk jacket. A "hold" tag with the name of an iconic American sportswear designer was attached to the sleeve. When I asked the manager why a leading sportswear designer would borrow a piece, she responded, "They come in here and rent things all the time." It was then that I realized that inspiration can be found anywhere, and that whether you're a fledgling dressmaker working from home or a well-known designer featured in top fashion magazines, an existing garment can give inspiration and serve as a starting point for a new project (as long as it doesn't violate someone else's copyright). Later that year I was able to use the rub-off method for a costume I designed at the Williamstown Theatre Festival in Massachusetts. I owned a vintage swing coat that I wanted to use, but the color wasn't right. I rubbed off the pattern from my swing coat and made a new one out of a 50s-era bedspread I found at a thrift store. The whole thing cost about $3.

After working in theatre for several years, I moved to Los Angeles and began work in film and TV. On my first day on the job as a patternmaker/fitter for the series *3rd Rock from the Sun*, the costume designer, Melina Root, handed me a crazy vintage fake fur parka with a red quilted lining. The jacket had become a signature piece for the Harry character and was going to get a lot of wear. She had purchased the exact fur and red quilted fabric and told me to make multiples of the parka (this would prove to be a common request). Melina and other designers taught me the valuable key to producing a lot of looks quickly: Start with something that already works, and build from that.

One day, the show's producer, Bonnie Turner, needed a formal gown for a red-carpet event. Since she wanted, above all else, to enjoy the evening and to be comfortable, she came to me

A pattern I used to make costumes for the Pat Nixon character, played by actress Joan Allen, in the film *Nixon*. A photocopied sketch by the late costume designer Richard Hornung can be seen on the envelope.

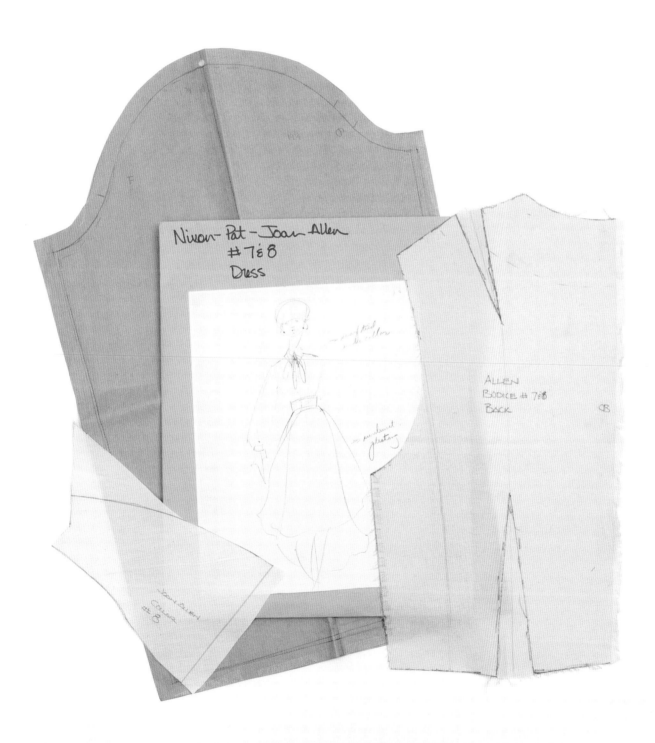

Nixon - Pat - Joan Allen
#7&8
Dress

ALLEN
BODICE #7&8
BACK   CB

with her favorite T-shirt and said, "Make me something that I can wear to the Emmys that feels like I'm wearing this, because I want to be able to hug people." Melina asked me to rub off the T-shirt and use the resulting pattern to create a dress out of an extraordinary silk chiffon. With just a little beading at the wrists and a simple black silk slip underneath, Bonnie looked elegant, understated, and chic, and—most importantly—felt comfortable.

I gained most of my experience with the rub-off techniques when I was asked to copy vintage garments for film and television. Fitting times are very limited and we considerably cut down research and development time by building "closets" for various characters. If we had a shape and size that worked, I'd create a rub-off pattern and then make multiple garments in different fabrics, slightly varying the details along the way. Using the rub-off techniques, I made and fit clothes for various actors and musicians, including Madonna, John Lithgow, John Travolta, Harry Belafonte, Roseanne, Joan Allen, Emma Thompson, and Bridget Fonda.

When working as a patternmaker/fitter for the late costume designer Richard Hornung for Oliver Stone's film *Nixon*, I needed to construct clothing for the Pat Nixon character, played by actress Joan Allen. For the first fitting, Richard and his assistants, Mark Bridges and Kimberly Adams, brought in vintage garments. Richard chose about five and we duplicated and modified them with the rub-off technique to create Joan's twenty-eight costumes. The information gleaned from the first fitting was the basis for all my work for the Pat Nixon character.

One of my proudest professional moments came just a few years later when Joan was nominated for an Oscar for Best Supporting Actress for her role in *Nixon*. The Fashion Institute of Design & Merchandising in Los Angeles held its annual exhibit, *The Art of Motion Picture Costume Design*, and to my delight some of the costumes I had made for the film were included. Shopping in a nearby fabric store, I overheard a conversation between two women who had seen the exhibit. One said to the other, "They used actual vintage pieces for Joan Allen in that film. I looked inside and you could tell from the construction." I simply smiled. I felt like a costume ninja, in and out with invisible skill and precision.

Recently, as I was cleaning out my great-grandmother's old sideboard, I came across a pile of sewing implements, mail-ordered sewing patterns, and newspaper clippings bundled together with slim strips of printed cotton. When I unrolled the clippings to decide which articles to keep, at first I couldn't decipher their relevance to my great-grandma. But as I looked through them I realized that they weren't just articles, but a pattern she had copied from a favorite blouse! Ironically, what I had studied and mastered as a professional was a household necessity to her, something so commonplace it didn't even bear repeating as a skill to be passed down to subsequent generations. In my great-grandmother's day, paper patterns had to be mail-ordered, so why bother going through the hassle if you had a perfectly good blouse that fit well? All you needed to do was trace a garment's shapes and make any necessary adjustments for whatever style you desired. When I realized the purpose of those scraps of paper, I felt a bond with my great-grandma that's difficult to explain.

A blouse pattern made by my great-grandmother, Dora Schoemann, from our local newspaper. The mail-order pattern envelope shown here was addressed to her from a pattern company in New York.

WHY LEARN THE RUB-OFF TECHNIQUE?

I can think of many good reasons for writing a book about copying garments using the rub-off technique. The first being that if you sew, you most likely already have in your sewing kit most of the materials needed. The second is that investigating the construction of vintage garments will give you an extremely valuable education in sewing techniques—I learned most of what I know about tailoring by performing countless alterations and duplications on vintage clothing.

However, the most compelling reason to learn the rub-off technique concerns the garments you already love to wear. We all have a favorite skirt or dress that we bought several seasons ago and that fits just right in every way—and no matter how hard we search, we can't find a similar one anywhere. In addition, we all have that one blouse we adore and want to have in every color, or at least be able to restyle it in interesting ways. Now you can! There's nothing more empowering or more sustainable than being able to re-create or redesign a favorite garment yourself.

11

CHAPTER 1 THE BASICS

THE RUB-OFF: Two Methods

As in any discipline, there's the traditional, academic approach—and the more improvisational, shorthand method, which develops from the daily practice of applying a skill to real-life situations. Most books about making flat patterns use the textbook approach to teach the science of patternmaking: Using set formulas you take measurements, fix them onto a flat plane and add the necessary curves based on standards designed to fit common body measurements. The more freehand and artistic approach (and my preferred method) involves **draping** fabric onto a dress form to create a pattern.

But, there is a third patternmaking technique that is often overlooked. This method—a closely guarded secret among fashion and costume professionals—duplicates various pieces and elements of an existing garment by making what's known in the industry as a "rub-off." But really, there's nothing so secret about it. A rub-off is simply a tracing that duplicates shapes by transferring the points from one plane (the garment) to corresponding points on another plane (a paper or fabric surface). In addition, the rub-off technique allows for investigation into the processes that were used to create the original garment. Rubbing-off provides a starting point for creating a garment that you know already works and saves you from having to reinvent the wheel. There are two different rub-off methods.

METHOD 1: The Paper Rub-Off

In this method, which is covered in step-by-step detail in Chapter 2 (see page 27), pins are placed through strategic points of the garment and into a piece of brown **kraft paper** underneath the garment. The kraft paper then serves as a pattern to re-create the original garment. It's a very accurate method of duplicating a pattern and is quite helpful when you need to make flat pattern pieces.

The paper rub-off method uses pins to outline a garment's shape onto kraft paper beneath it, creating an accurate duplicate.

METHOD 2: The Fabric Rub-Off

This method, explained in depth in Chapter 3 (see page 65), differs from the paper rub-off in that muslin (the most common fabric to use) or other tracing fabric is draped around the shape of the garment, either because its shape prevents it from being laid flat for tracing or because pinning into the original could cause damage. Fabric is draped over the garment, the seam lines are traced, and any darts or junctures—along with other pattern pieces—are noted. The fabric rub-off works especially well for patterning three-dimensional shapes like bags and other accessories. Although sometimes not quite as accurate as the paper rub-off, fabric is easier to manipulate than paper and allows you to fit the garment during the rub-off process. Because of this, you'll be able to more closely approximate style features like **gathers** and **pleats**. In addition, this method is less likely to damage the source garment, since you're only pinning through its seams, making it quite useful when patterning a garment (a historical piece, for example) that can't be altered in any way. It also dramatically reduces cutting time, leaving more time for fitting and finishing, as it eliminates much of the documentation found on multiple-use patterns. If you make a fabric rub-off of something that you'll only need one of, then you don't actually need to make a paper pattern at all; you simply lay out the fabric pattern on the fabric from which you'll be making the new garment and the fabric-on-fabric texture eliminates the need for excessive pinning or weighting of the pattern. If, however, you'll be making multiples or need to alter the pattern in any way, you'll have to trace the fabric pattern onto kraft paper using a **needle wheel**. This allows you to "true up" the pattern more easily, using pencil and rulers, and provides a crisp pattern that can be used multiple times.

You can decide which method is most comfortable and works best for you or your project. If I know that the garment I'm duplicating fits the wearer well, won't need any alteration in size or style, and that I'll want or need multiples of it, I use the paper rub-off method because it'll give me a very accurate multiple-use pattern with lots of information that can easily be passed on to others. If, however, I need to re-create a one-off garment in a hurry and know that I'll be sewing it myself, I use the fabric method.

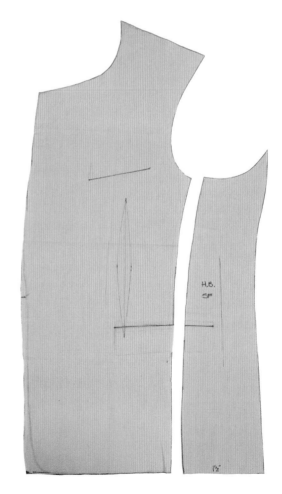

The fabric rub-off method involves draping muslin, or other tracing fabric, over a garment and tracing its seam lines onto the surface of the fabric, creating a quick and easy pattern. The pattern can then be transferred to kraft paper, if needed. This pattern is a rub-off I made for a costume for Harry Belafonte in the film *White Man's Burden*.

TOOLS AND EQUIPMENT

If you've been sewing for a while, the tools needed for rub-off projects are materials you probably already have on hand. If not, obtaining these materials will make your sewing much easier! As with any craft, there are always larger, fancier, and more professional versions of all of the tools and supplies I list here. These are great if you have the space and budget, but you can rub off just as effectively with basic sewing tools and materials.

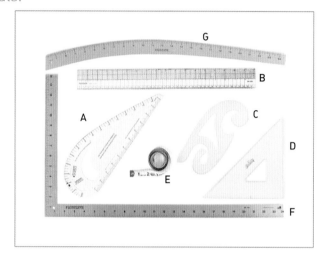

Measuring tools are used to measure not only the human form but also the garment you're duplicating and the pattern that will be created.

A Design curve to create smooth armholes, sleeve caps, and necklines

B **Gridded ruler** to find perpendicular lines, **bias**, and to easily measure **seam allowances**

C **French curve** to make smooth, smaller curves like those for pockets or collars

D Plastic 45/90° square to find square **angles** and the bias grain of fabric

E Tape measure to measure the body, curved seams, or pattern pieces

F **Yardstick** or large metal ruler to create a long, straight lines and for measuring the distance of a hem from the ground

G Hip curve for blending more gradual curves

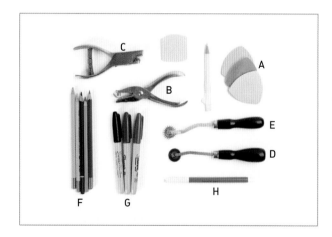

Marking tools help you to create new patterns by identifying seam lines on the fabric rub-off patterns, to "connect the pin dots" in a paper rub-off pattern, and to establish style elements, notches, and seam allowances.

A **Tailor's chalk** (wax is best) to mark notches, hems, or other temporary lines

B Hole punch to make holes in your patterns for hanging or marking dots, which identify matching areas on pattern pieces

C Pattern notcher to make clean, uniform notches on a paper pattern

D **Tracing wheel** to transfer marks from a paper surface to a fabric surface

E Needle wheel to transfer marks from a fabric surface to a paper surface

F Pencils to draw lines on paper patterns

G Markers to ink your final pattern shape and mark corrections

H Invisible marker to make rub-offs of delicate garments (they avoid permanent damage on a garment)

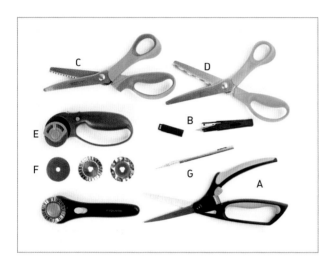

These are my favorite tools for cutting various materials, from fabric and paper to thread.

Ⓐ Spring-handle shears to cut fabric

Ⓑ Thread snips to cut threads as you sew

Ⓒ Pinking shears to finish raw fabric edges without adding bulk

Ⓓ Wave shears to create decorative edges

Ⓔ Rotary cutter to speed up the cutting process

Ⓕ Rotary cutter blades for straight and decorative edges

Ⓖ X-Acto knife to cut out areas of paper to make templates

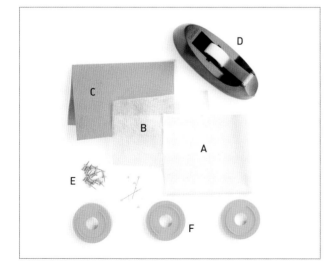

You'll need these patterning supplies to make your own patterns. They can be purchased at local craft and office supply stores or online.

Ⓐ Lightweight **muslin** (or other tracing fabric) to drape over objects

Ⓑ Do-Sew™, a commercially available transparent patterning material that looks like **interfacing** without the "glue" on it

Ⓒ Brown kraft paper to create paper patterns

Ⓓ ¾-inch tape and dispenser (to affix additional paper to enlarge patterns)

Ⓔ Aluminum push-pins and straight pins to trace a garment and anchor it to a work surface

Ⓕ Pattern weights to hold the garment while cutting

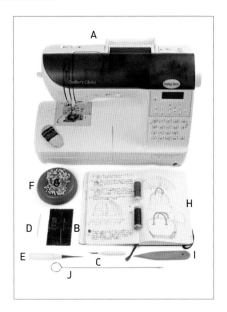

These are the basic sewing tools needed to sew the garment projects. Some are necessities (machine, needles, seam ripper, pins); others are tricks of the trade (awl, toothpicks, point and loop turners). Use a journal to make notes about techniques so you can avoid having to test an idea over and over.

A Sewing machine

B Hand-sewing needles to finish hems, **facings**, buttons, and other closures

C **Seam ripper** to remove unwanted stitches

D Toothpicks to use as spacers when sewing on buttons

E **Awl** to make holes, or to use as a pushing tool

F Pincushion to hold pins

G Straight pins to hold the work before sewing

H Sewing journal to record observations and calculations

I **Point turner** to push out the points of corners

J Loop turner to aid in turning narrow tubes

Proper pressing is the key to sewing success. These tools make pressing any surface easier and quicker, resulting in a better-looking finished garment.

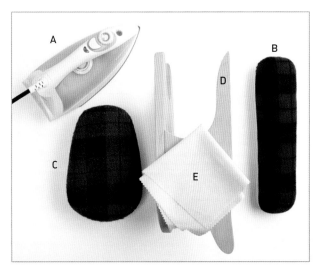

A Iron

Ironing board (not pictured)

B **Sleeve board** or roll— to **press open** small areas

C **Pressing ham** to press curved surfaces

D Tailor's board to press open points or very narrow edges

E Muslin scrap to use as a **pressing cloth**

Buying fabric for your project is only the first step. You'll also need inner structure or finishing items to give the garment a polished look.

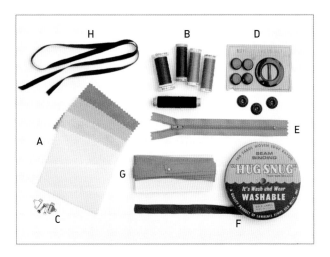

A Interfacings to add stability to facings and waistbands

B Thread to match chosen fabrics

C Hooks and eyes/bars for closures

D Buttons

E Zippers

F Seam binding to finish off **hems**

G Bias tape to finish off other raw edges

H **Twill tape** to stabilize edges that may stretch out

CHOOSING THE RIGHT PINS

Depending on the source garment's fabric and its condition, you can use anything from aluminum push-pins and quilting straight pins to **silk pins**. Each of these pins makes a different-sized hole, so you'll need to determine what the fabric can withstand. I recommend using the most delicate pin possible for the project. If you're working with a very old or deteriorating original fabric, you'll obviously want to use the thinnest, most delicate pin you can find—and use them sparingly. If you're working with leather, fake fur, or a heavy woolen fabric, then quilting straight pins or aluminum push-pins are fine. If you have any doubts, err on the side of caution.

Pins: An aluminum push-pin, quilting straight pin, and silk pin.

FABRIC

When rubbing off, the *most important* thing to remember before you begin your project is that you'll obtain much better results if you make your copy in the same fabric as the source garment. Of course, there are always exceptions—and it's always fun to experiment—but as a general rule, I recommend working with a fabric similar in type to the original. This section reviews two of the most common types of fabric and grain lines.

Knit fabric consists of fibers looped together in interlocking rows.

Knits vs. Wovens

Knitted fabric is made by looping fibers together in rows. It's very drapey and flexible. **Woven** fabric is made by weaving fibers in a gridded pattern. It has less "give" and is generally sturdier, depending on its density.

Grain Lines

Another very important feature of fabric is its grain line. Fabric that falls on the **straight of grain** hangs up and down. A fabric's straight of grain runs parallel to the **selvage** edge of the piece of fabric. Fabric that falls on the bias is very flexible and drapey and molds to the body. The bias of a fabric is found by marking a line at a forty-five-degree angle to the selvage edge. Fabric that's cut on the **cross grain** is less drapey and more bouncy and buoyant. The **cross grain** is the direction that runs perpendicular to the selvage edge of the fabric.

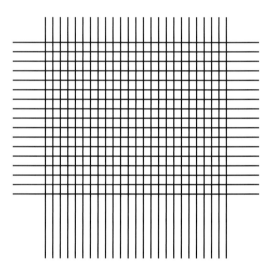

Woven fabric is made with two sets of perpendicular threads that are woven under and over each other.

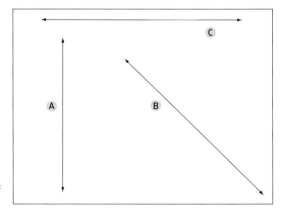

This diagram shows the various grain lines in fabric: the Ⓐ straight of grain, Ⓑ bias, and Ⓒ cross grain.

This cotton wrap skirt variation (see page 57) was cut on the straight of grain.

ESTIMATING YARDAGE

You can estimate the yardage you'll need for a project by measuring the length of the individual pattern pieces and then adding them together. Remember, more than one pattern piece will usually fit across the width of the fabric; as a result, some pieces will be nested together. You can also lay out pattern pieces with the grain lines running in the correct directions and measure the length you'll need for the garment.

After reading yardage charts found on the back of commercial patterns you'll quickly see that there's no such thing as a standard yardage for every skirt, blouse, or dress. Factors that need to be taken into account when estimating yardage include (1) the size of the individual pattern pieces, (2) the width of the fabric you're using, (3) the grain lines of each piece, (4) the print on the fabric, and (5) the direction of a fabric's **nap**, if needed. Nap is a piled surface on the fabric, as is found on piled velvet or corduroy. Light reflects differently depending on whether the nap runs up or down, so it's essential that each pattern piece for the garment is laid out with the nap running in the same direction. The following steps will give you an accurate estimate as to how much fabric yardage you'll need for your rub-off project:

1 Measure the width of the fabric you're planning to use and make a notation on your work surface with a piece of tape or by laying out a ruler or tape measure. The majority of fashion fabrics are 45 inches or 60 inches wide.

2 Lay all the pattern pieces out with the grain lines running in the same direction (parallel to the length of the fabric).

3 Place the larger pieces first and then fit the smaller pieces around the larger ones to conserve fabric. Don't forget to include any belts, facings, cuffs, collars, or other small pieces.

4 Once you have all of the pieces nested together within the fabric width, measure the length of all the pieces together. The calculation is the yardage you'll need to purchase. Make a note of it, as you may need to use it again in the future.

5 If the fabric is napped or has a design repeat that needs to be matched, add an extra 10 percent to the total estimate. For large designs that repeat less often, add 50 percent.

Over time these calculations will become second nature to you. I often just simply measure a rough area of the torso and the estimated length of a sleeve or skirt—or both—and add them together, figuring in that the facings and other small pieces can be nested around the larger pieces. You can calculate the yardage for a bias skirt by measuring the diagonal length of the skirt. Do this by measuring from the waist on one side of the body diagonally across the legs to where the hem will be, or if you already have the pattern piece, just measure the length of the pattern running diagonally from the top of one side to the bottom of the other.

TAKING MEASUREMENTS

Before you begin any custom-sewing project, you need to take measurements, especially if you plan to alter the pattern after you make it. Make sure you take measurements over the type of underwear you, or the wearer, will be wearing with the garment. Wear something close-fitting and measure **1** around the fullest part of the bust, **2** around the waist at the belly button and, **3** around the fullest part of the hips. Also take any other measurements you may need, such as from the waist to above the knee, waist to the knee, waist to below the knee, waist to the ankle, and waist to the floor. If you're making a jacket or a blouse, you'll want to measure the sleeve length from the shoulder to the wrist. Custom-made clothing shops have extensive measurement sheets that you may want to check out.

Take measurements that will correspond to the area of the body for which you'll be making the garment. If you'll make other projects for the same person in the future, you may want to have all these measurements. (Hint: Some people really hate to be measured, so you may want to adjust accordingly—no more than you need to make the garment, but enough so you don't have to ask the person to be measured repeatedly. Plan ahead for which measurements you'll need.)

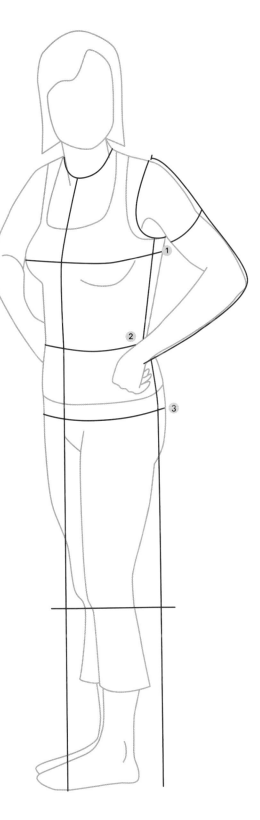

SEWING ESSENTIALS

There are a few basic principles that are important to know when sewing without a commercial pattern and instructions. Once you master these, you can apply them in many different situations. The following techniques are the foundation for many of the sewing steps we'll cover in this book.

Aside from maintaining consistency within the stitching, the most important, underlying step that will determine how polished a finished garment will look is pressing. As you move on to each new step, the garment needs to be properly pressed to ensure a smooth, well-constructed garment. Skip this important step and the seams, which need to be incorporated into each other, will not join nicely and will create a clunky, less elegant-looking garment.

Concave Curves

If you're sewing a concave curve, such as a neckline or an armhole facing, you'll need to clip and trim the seam allowances at regular intervals. You'll then need to press the seam allowance open on a tailor's board so when the facing is turned right side out, the excess seam allowance can open and spread out. This will allow the seam to be pressed smoothly from the right side and allow the facing to lie nicely without rolling to one side. Press the seam first from the inside of the seam allowance to create a crisp seam and then from the right side of the finished garment to create a nice, finished edge.

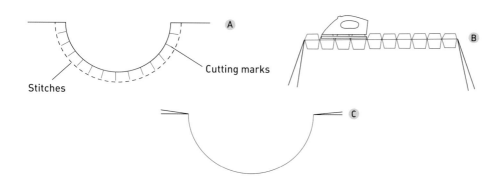

Stitches

Cutting marks

A A concave curve illustrating stitches and cutting marks. **B** Press the concave curve open on a tailor's board. The clips you've made allow you to press the seam open flat and then for it to spread when the piece is turned right side out. **C** If a concave curve is clipped properly, the outside edge will make a smooth curve; if not, go back and clip where needed.

Convex Curves

If you're sewing a convex curve, such as a rounded collar or cuff, you'll need to trim the seam allowance and then remove the excess fabric in the seam by cutting little **notches** at intervals along the curve. This will allow the seam allowance to be turned and pressed and not wrinkle and fold in on itself, which adds bulk to the seam. If clipped properly, the edge should make a smooth curve; if it's bumpy, go back and notch some more to remove the excess fabric.

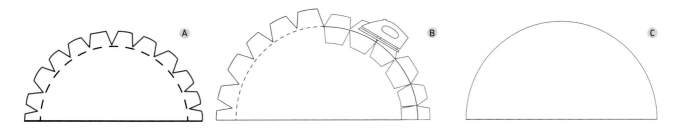

(A) A convex curve notched. (B) Use a pressing ham or tailor's board to press seams open. (C) Turn and press.

Corners

When sewing a corner, such as a collar or waistband, you'll need to trim the corner and press the seam open. Don't sew all the way to the corner, pivot the needle in the fabric and turn at a 90-degree angle. Doing so will result in a corner that's too pointed and narrow—not pretty. The nicest-looking corners have a slight **miter** at the point. To achieve this, sew within two stitches of the corner and then make two stitches across it before continuing around to the other side. Trim around the piece, press it open, and then turn and press again to give it a nice, smooth edge.

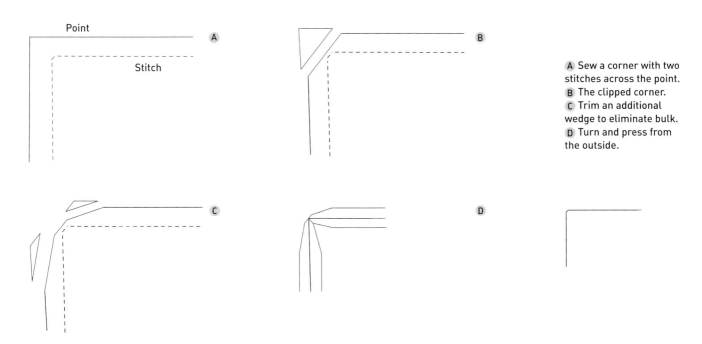

(A) Sew a corner with two stitches across the point.
(B) The clipped corner.
(C) Trim an additional wedge to eliminate bulk.
(D) Turn and press from the outside.

CHAPTER 2

PATTERNING SKIRTS

THE SOURCE SKIRT

We'll begin our lessons in the rub-off technique with a skirt, as it's the simplest garment to pattern and sew. The source skirt used in this project is a classic, wool pencil skirt that has a straight shape with no flare, and is constructed with only four pieces: a front, two back halves, and a waistband. Four darts shape the waist, a kick pleat on the center back seam allows for ease of movement, and a traditional waistband laps over and buttons with a side zipper. There's also a small, rounded patch pocket on the front, which I took out for simplicity; however, it is added back in the Casual Denim Skirt variation (see page 49).

I chose this basic skirt not only for its simplicity, but because it's a classic shape that can take on a variety of looks, depending on the fit and accessories, and can be duplicated in many different fabrics. As you'll see on pages 47–63, the pattern for this narrow, fitted skirt can be altered into varying degrees of fullness to create an entire wardrobe of shapes, from straight and A-line to a circle.

The simplicity of the source skirt pattern lends itself to a vast array of shape variations. Each new skirt pattern can continue to evolve into something further from its original shape. For our first rub-off project, I've chosen the paper method, which is a bit quicker and easier to understand.

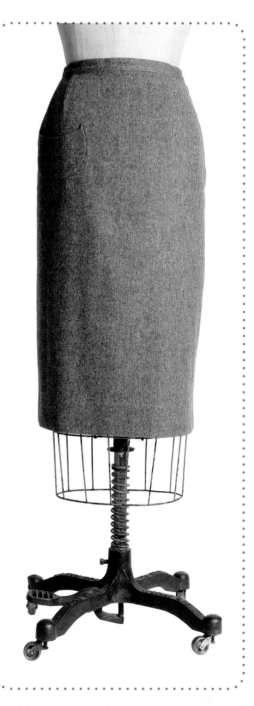

The kick pleat.

The pocket and waistband.

Our vintage source pencil skirt.

The Paper Rub-Off Method

All that's needed for the paper rub-off method is a work surface that can be pinned into. I've used a variety of surfaces in my career, including large, gridded cardboard cutting boards that can be found in most fabric stores. Eventually, I permanently covered my cutting table with 2 x 4–foot acoustic ceiling tiles purchased from a home improvement store. I then covered the tiles with kraft paper, which keeps the surface nice and tidy. I can lay out my patterning paper and pin through the garment and into the paper and table. If you don't want to cover an entire table, cover a single acoustical tile with kraft paper or use a folding gridded cardboard cutting mat—both can easily be stored under a bed or in a closet when not in use. Once you have a work surface, you're ready to begin.

An acoustic ceiling tile covered with kraft paper.

The process of tracing a garment is exactly what it sounds like. Remember tracing around your hand or another object as a child and using the tracing in an art or craft project? You were simply transferring information from one plane to another plane. The same principles are applied for the paper rub-off. In areas where you're able to lay the garment out flat and trace around it with a pencil, you do just that. The difficulty comes when you need to trace around an entire piece of a garment that's connected to another piece. These areas are delineated by placing pins through the line you want to trace into the paper underneath. By doing this, you're transferring the information from one plane (the source garment) to another plane (the paper).

THE SKIRT FRONT

Cut a piece of kraft paper that will easily accommodate the skirt you're patterning. Since the individual pieces that make up the source skirt are symmetrical, they can be patterned on the fold. Always start with the largest areas first and work toward the smallest so that you'll use your paper wisely.

1 Begin at the far-left side of the paper and make a straight vertical line that's longer than the total length of the skirt. At the bottom of the line, create an L-shape by drawing a second line perpendicular to the first. These are the lines to which you'll be anchoring the skirt, ensuring that it stays on the straight of grain (see **A**).

2 Fold the skirt down the **center front** (commonly abbreviated as CF). Pin the side seams together and make sure the two sides are even.

3 Place the garment on your work surface and pin it to the vertical line. This will represent the center front (see **B**).

4 After you've anchored the skirt along the center front line, smooth it across the paper, adjusting any wrinkles as you go. Place a few pins into the grain line of the fabric to keep your work square and to keep from having to correct any skewing of the pattern later. In our source skirt the grain line runs down the center front.

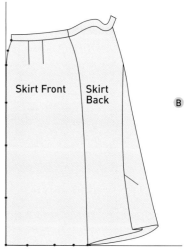

A Our L-shape lines. **B** The skirt folded down its center front line and pinned to the vertical line on the paper.

5 Continue to smooth the skirt and pin the outer edges of the front, making sure to keep the grain lines straight and square. Continue all around the piece, making sure that you're not creating wrinkles in the skirt. If you don't take this precaution, the duplicate skirt may be much smaller than the original. Mark any other features, such as closures or junctures, as you go. For now, use pins to document the position of the darts (see C). We'll be adding the darts into the pattern later (see page 34) and will create a separate pattern for the waistband (see page 32).

THE SKIRT BACK

After you've pinned all of the seam lines and darts, remove the pins and set the paper pattern piece aside. Take a new sheet of kraft paper and lay it on your work surface.

1 Begin by determining the straight of grain. In our source skirt, the straight of grain is on the **center back** seam (commonly abbreviated as CB), which is usually the case for most skirts. Fold the skirt back and in half and pin the side seams. Then draw a backwards L-shape on your sheet of paper and pin the skirt to it (see D).

2 Continue pinning and marking as you did for the skirt front, making notations of the **darts**, zipper, and any pleats.

3 Our source skirt has a kick pleat at the center back seam. Measure the depth of the kick pleat with your ruler to determine how much fabric to add to the seam to pattern the pleat. Notice how far the pleat extends up and into the center back seam and make a mark at this level. This is the top of your pleat. Now, using your gridded ruler, measure the distance you determined to be the width of the pleat from the center back seam and draw in a new line parallel to the center back seam. This is the outer edge of your kick pleat. Determine the angle of the top of the pleat by measuring up from the hem at the inner and outer edges of the pleat. Transfer those measurements to the new pleat line on the paper as shown in the illustration E. You'll add these details into the paper pattern piece in the next step. After this piece is marked, set it aside and move on to the waistband.

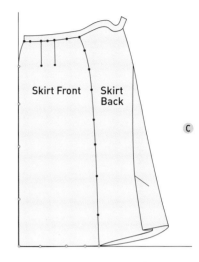

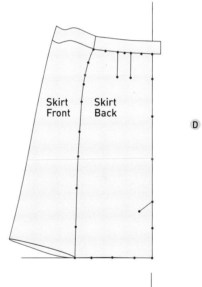

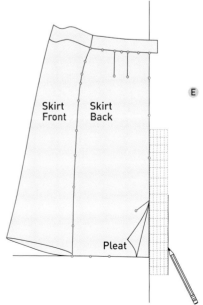

C The skirt front pinned all around its edges at each curve and corner. D The skirt back pinned along the vertical line on the paper. E The new pleat measurement drawn in.

THE WAISTBAND

To trace a pattern for the waistband you can use the same pinning technique described in the previous steps of the skirt front and back. If the waistband is a simple rectangle and completely symmetrical all the way around, you can simply measure its overall length and width and draw it onto a sheet of kraft paper using a clear gridded ruler.

Begin by drawing a straight, horizontal line, which will serve as your base line, along the bottom of the paper. Take the measurement of the entire waist from one edge of the zipper all the way around to the other edge. Mark these end points on the line and draw in perpendicular lines to create the outer edges of your rectangle. Measure how much of the waistband overlaps past the zipper. Then measure from the outer edge of your waistband rectangle and mark a line that's perpendicular to the base line. Now draw another straight line at the top of the rectangle to create the top of the waistband. Label the overlap extension so that you'll know exactly where to pin the waistband to the skirt (this overlap will not be pinned to the skirt, but will be left over when the skirt is pinned to the waistband). You'll notice that the ends of the button placket in the source skirt are tapered. To account for this detail, fold the paper waistband pattern in half. Find the center of the end line and angle it away from the center point at a 45-degree angle. Traditionally, side zippers are applied to the left side and lap toward the back (see pages 52–53 of the Wool Tweed Pencil Skirt variation for a description of how to apply a lapped zipper). In this project we'll be placing the zipper in the center, which, in addition to being easier, is also a less conspicuous placement.

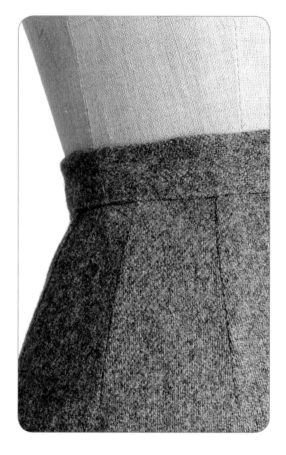

This waistband has a tapered overlap, which is made by folding the paper in half, finding the center of the end line, and drawing tapering lines away from the enter point at 45-degree angles.

After you've transferred all of your pin marks to the paper, take a ruler and pencil and begin to connect the pin holes to make the paper skirt pattern (see A). Use a **curve tool** to draw the line of the hip and the top of the skirt. Draw the lines lightly, as you're just sketching at this point—we'll be changing some of them to add in darts and seam allowances later (see B).

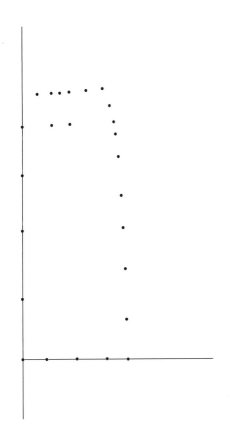

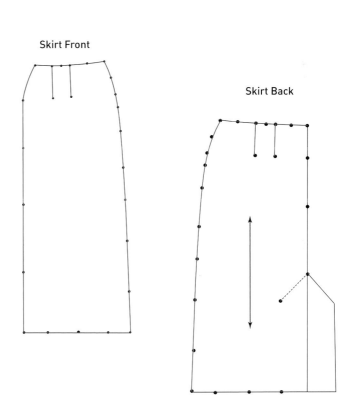

Skirt Front

Skirt Back

A The pin holes that will become the paper skirt pattern.

B The traced lines of skirt front and back before correcting the darts.

ADDING AND ADJUSTING DART MEASUREMENTS

If your source skirt has darts, examine them from the inside. Because we've copied the finished dimensions of the skirt so far, we need to add back to the pattern the amount of fabric that has been sewn out of the darts. If you don't do this and just draw a dart over the finished line you copied, the duplicate garment will be too small.

1 Take a tape measure or ruler and measure the depth and length of each dart (see C). In our case, each dart is 1 inch. Make notes of the measurements. I have eliminated two darts on either side in order to fit on a modern figure (see "Altering Vintage Garments for a Modern Fit" on page 35). When pinning the skirt front during tracing, the skirt cannot be pinned to the center front seam and remain smooth and flat. Instead, it pulls away from the vertical line on the paper toward the top edge. When creating the pattern for the source skirt, I added this dimension back into the center front seam. This amount is equivalent to one of the darts. Draw the amount back into the skirt pattern as seen in illustration **D**. The original finished waist measurement is maintained, but the fullness is redistributed from across the abdomen and the small of the back to the hips at the side seams. **Note:** The line with two arrows on the skirt front illustration represents that the fabric needs to be cut on the fold.

2 Use the same method for the skirt back.

3 Darts should be trued up, or redrawn, so the lines are straight and the center line falls on the straight of grain. The depth of the dart should then be marked at the top. **Truing up** is a term that's often used in patternmaking and refers to any time you refine your rough initial sketch by measuring and using straight edges and curves for a more elegant, precise line.

4 Make a notation onto the center front pattern to remind you that the piece needs to be cut on the fold.

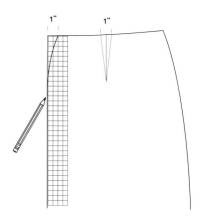

C Measuring the size of the darts on the skirt front.

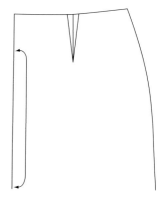

D The skirt front pattern adjusted with only one dart.

ALTERING VINTAGE GARMENTS FOR A MODERN FIT

One of the most common fitting problems when rubbing off vintage source garments is a discrepancy between the period's silhouette and today's modern body. If you like to wear girdles with garter belts and bullet bras, then by all means go for the fit of the period silhouette. However, if you plan to wear modern undergarments with your creation, then the most common and helpful alteration is to soften the severe, nipped-in waist.

As you can see with our source skirt in this project, there is a charming overabundance of darts, which were used to achieve the nipped-in waist favored by the pre–bra-burning generation. If you account for the removal of these darts by adding the measurements to the side or back seams, you'll achieve fullness around the belly area that is generally considered unflattering on the modern body. The best fix for this is to eliminate one of the darts on each side of the front waist. How do you know which dart to eliminate? Keep the darts closest to a princess line on each side—the darts that are the closest to the center in the pattern. You can even split the difference by redrawing a single dart between the old ones, if it's a more pleasing distribution. You would then adjust the pattern to compensate for the extra fabric in the waist dimension by removing the same amount from the side seams, or by just leaving the curve in the side seam that's created in the rub-off from the former dart. For more information, see "Adding and Adjusting Dart Measurements" on page 34.

Two darts may still work in the back, depending on the fullness the wearer may need in the finished garment. If your vintage source garment has the same overly puffy area across the seat, then remove a dart on each side of the waist in the back as well.

LABELING THE PATTERN PIECES

You'll need to label each of your pattern pieces with the garment name, piece name, any special instructions, and placement of the zippers, pockets, and darts. You can make as many, or as few, notations as you think will be helpful to you. Just remember that it's much easier to tell the pieces apart and to determine what should be sewn to what with the pattern attached, than it is when you take the pattern away. You can easily get confused if you haven't given yourself some clues at this stage.

1 Include any notches or other notations that will guide you in the sewing or identification of the individual pieces (see E). Standard notching is one notch for the center front, two for the side front (SF), and so on, making your way around to the center back.

2 If you would like to make any changes to the size or style of the skirt, do it now, before you add seam allowances. If you're duplicating a source garment directly, compare it to the measurements of the pattern. Continue marking each remaining piece until you have your new pattern. At this point you have what is called a basic "block" or "sloper."

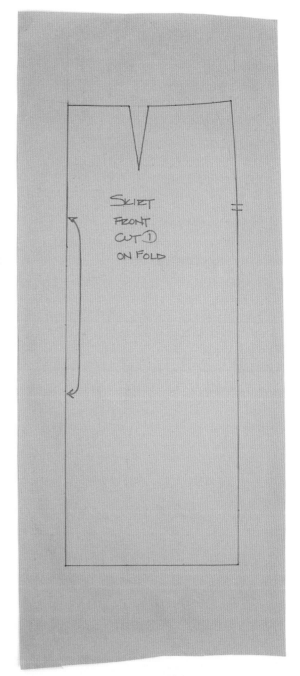

E Grain line, notches, and cutting instructions labeled on the pattern.

Notches are just small marks that are made onto a pattern and then transferred to the cut fabric pieces. Their job is to:

★ Identify individual pattern pieces
★ Indicate the front and back sides of a sleeve
★ Alert the stitcher to a different seam allowance than is used throughout the rest of the garment
★ Specify the placement of buttons, darts, or other style features
★ Delineate exact connection points between two garment pieces to maintain accuracy in the distribution of fullness (when marking a sleeve cap, for example, you'll want to make notches where the sleeve cap is attached to the armhole)

Notches are made either by making a simple V or by using a special tool called a **pattern notcher**. A pattern notcher is like a hole punch in that it leaves a little opening in the paper pattern through which you can then mark the fabric. Using notches may seem time-consuming at first, but they'll save you lots of time, as they alert you to common mistakes like sewing a sleeve in backward. If you learn how to use notches, they'll quickly become second nature and save you hours of frustration.

A pattern notcher allows you to quickly cut out shapes that can then be marked through like a stencil.

ALTERING THE SKIRT PATTERN

At this stage you should add any additional length or width you'll need to alter the pattern for fit. Length is easy. For width I find that in most cases you can simply increase the seam allowance in the side seams or center back seams. If you need to add more than a couple of inches, however, you run the risk of the side seams becoming more distorted in your pattern. Therefore, a good rule of thumb is that if you need to add more than ½ inch to the side seams or 1 inch total per piece, you'll need to "slash and spread" the pattern in order to maintain the integrity of the darts or other style features.

Slashing and spreading is a way to add dimension to the pattern piece from the interior instead of the exterior lines. You can either use the pattern you just made, or if you'd like to keep a copy of the pattern at its original size, you can use a needle wheel to make a copy (see F). If you need to add width, divide each pattern piece in half with a vertical pencil line. If you need to add length, divide the pattern piece with a horizontal line. Often, you will need to do both. After you divide the pattern into halves or quarters, cut the pieces apart and arrange them on a separate piece of paper, spreading them enough to reach the new dimension you need to fit the person you're sewing for. When you've enlarged the pattern to your liking, tape the pieces down to create a new, larger pattern piece.

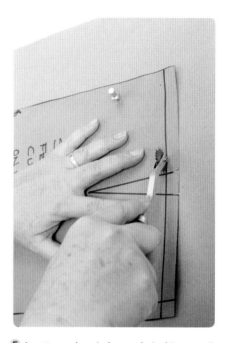

F A pattern piece being copied with a needle wheel.

1 First determine how much needs to be added to each pattern piece by taking the desired measurement and subtracting the measurement from the original. For example, if you're duplicating a skirt that fits a friend who has a 35-inch hip measurement and you have a 39-inch hip, you would subtract 35 from 39, which leaves you with a difference of 4 inches. You would also need to take into account that you don't want the skirt to be skintight, so you'd need to build some **ease** into the garment. Therefore, you might add anywhere from 1 to 3 inches to the 4 inches, depending on the style of the skirt. Our source skirt is fitted but not upholstered to the body, so I would add 2 inches of ease, which can easily be adjusted during a fitting.

2 Cut along the lines within the pattern and "spread" the piece until it fits the measurement of the wearer.

3 Tape the spread-out pattern pieces to the measured line on the second paper, and you have an expanded pattern piece (see G).

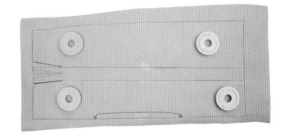

G The new slashed-and-spread pattern.

By these calculations I would then need to add a total of 6 inches to the entire pattern in order to adjust the garment properly. This amount needs to be divided by the total number of pieces. In this case, there are two halves for the front and two halves for the back, for a total of four pieces. Since 6 divided by 4 is 1½, I would add 1½ inches to each pattern piece in order to get the correct dimensions to distribute the 6 inches evenly among the four pieces.

After you've altered the pattern for size, determine whether to alter it for style, to create new seam lines, or to divide the pattern pieces to create blocks of color or other elements of visual interest. The possibilities are endless, so this is where your creativity can really come to life. A few variations of what can be done to create new patterns from the simple sloper of the source skirt are shown on pages 47–63.

In addition, there are many excellent books that can spark your imagination when adding these kinds of details to your garment; my favorite is *The Art of Manipulating Fabric* by Colette Wolff. When seeking inspiration, I also hunt through used bookstores for vintage magazines and patternmaking, fashion, and costume books.

ADDING SEAM ALLOWANCES

After you've finalized your patterns, you need to add seam allowances all the way around. Using your clear gridded ruler, measure around the edges of all the pattern pieces and add the desired seam allowances with a pencil or marker (see **H**).

Most commercial patterns come with a ⅝-inch seam allowance. If that's comfortable for you, then add it to your pattern pieces. I tend to use ½-inch seam allowances if I'm confident in the fit, since much of the seam allowance tends to be clipped away. In apparel industry production, the price of fabric and the reduction of trimming steps are major concerns, so some finished garments might have as little as ¼-inch seam allowance. In costume construction it's customary to leave generous seam allowances wherever possible for future modifications of the garment.

The costume construction approach may be useful to you in certain situations. It's always nice to have a generous seam allowance on side seams or center back seams if you're sewing for someone who's likely to fluctuate in size, or for someone whose measurements were taken by another person. You also may be asked to create a garment for someone you won't have an opportunity to fit. It's a good idea to factor in some room for adjustment, for example, when creating dresses for multiple bridesmaids, who many times give their measurements remotely and who are then fitted at the last minute before the wedding.

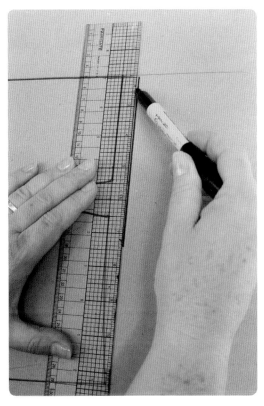

H Adding seam allowances is easy with a clear gridded ruler.

Now that you've finished your pattern, it's time to cut the fabric. First, prewash or dry clean the fabric to avoid any surprise shrinkage that may occur when the finished skirt is first laundered.

1 Lay out the fabric on a large table and fold it in half lengthwise (see A). The only exception to this instruction is if you're cutting a fabric with a directional nap or pattern that needs to be accounted for. In that case, cut each piece individually, matching up the stripes or other dominant graphic elements (see "Cutting and Sewing To Match Stripes or Patterns" on page 56). Begin with your largest piece and work around the garment, cutting piece by piece and making pencil guidelines onto the pattern as you go. When matching stripes, you must also take into account the seam allowances and make sure the stripes intersect where the garment will be sewn together—not at the edge from which you're cutting. Although this takes a little extra time when laying out the fabric, it makes all the difference for a polished look in the finished skirt.

2 Once you've laid out your fabric and determined that it's straight without any drag lines, begin to place your pattern pieces. Start by noting the grain lines of each individual piece and place any pieces to be cut on the fold first—for this skirt I placed the center front pattern piece on the fold. Then place the next-largest piece—in this case the back pattern piece. Check that you've placed the patterns on the straight of grain by measuring the distance from the edge of the fabric to the grain line arrows at both ends.

3 When you're certain that all the pieces are placed correctly, pin the paper pattern to the fabric. If you're using a rotary cutter and a cutting mat, place fabric weights onto the pattern pieces (see B).

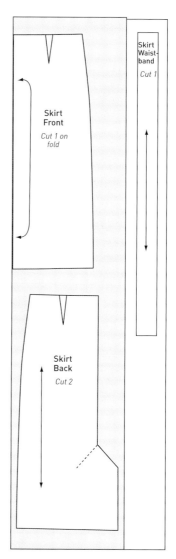

A The skirt pattern pieces laid out with the grain line running parallel to the selvage edge. The gray section represents the folded, outside, side of the fabric. The white section represents the inside. Place on the folded part of the fabric (the gray part) the pattern pieces that either (1) will be cut on the fold or (2) those in which two pieces will be cut. For the patterns in which only one piece will be cut, place them on the single layer of fabric (the white part). (This method will be used in all the cutting sections throughout the book).

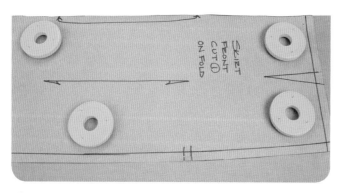

B The paper pattern with weights.

ROTARY CUTTERS

For a long time I was hesitant about using a rotary cutter for garment construction, but after working in a production environment I became sold on its speed. It's one of the most significant changes in sewing in the last twenty years, and it's very rare now for me to cut anything without it. Eliminating the tedious pinning of a pattern to the fabric will also eliminate a huge percentage of time spent at the cutting stage, which can be a great motivation to begin a new project. I especially like to have a large cutting mat set up in a dedicated sewing space. It makes the idea of starting a new project much more appealing. Once you've become proficient with a rotary cutter, you can use it to cut multiple garments simultaneously.

4 Cut out all the fabric pieces and then mark your notches, darts, and any other notations you've made to the pattern (see **C**). This is a vital step in saving time later. Take a marking pencil or tailor's chalk and mark the notches on both pieces of the fabric. Mark the darts with a tracing wheel (see **D**).

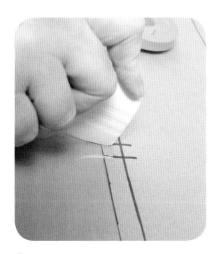

C Marking notches with tailor's chalk.

D Marking the darts with a tracing wheel.

Just as there is a logic to cutting a garment by placing and cutting the largest pattern pieces first and then nesting the smaller pieces around the bigger pieces in order to conserve fabric, there is a logic to sewing your garment in a certain order. I like to cut from large to small, but sew from small to large. Sew any features within a pattern piece while it's still flat and easy to handle. Then, when all the pieces have their individual components in place, sew the separate pieces together until finally, you're sewing larger groups of pieces.

STITCHING THE DARTS

To stitch darts, pin the dart starting at the point and then upward. Then sew it from the top and down, stopping just before you reach the bottom point (see **A**). As you remove the fabric from the sewing machine, raise the presser foot and pull the piece out by the bottom of the dart, making a "tail" of both threads. Leave the tail about four inches long, cut the threads, take both threads, and tie a knot at the bottom of the dart. This makes a beautiful, stable dart every time (see **B**). Tips like these will make a beautiful finish. You could also sew a single reverse stitch at the beginning and end of the dart.

A A pinned dart. **B** A sewn dart.

INSERTING THE ZIPPER

Sometimes a souce skirt will have a side zip, usually on the left side, lapped toward the back. I've changed the placement of the zipper in this project because I like the smooth, uninterrupted line on the side seams you obtain when the zipper is moved to the back. For an example of how to apply a lapped zipper, see "Hand Finishing a Lapped Zipper" on page 52–53.

1 Begin by stitching the center back seam from the top using a large basting-length stitch on your sewing machine (usually 4–5 millimeters) until you reach the bottom of the zipper area (see **C**). Then change the stitch length to normal (usually 2.5–3 millimeters) and continue stitching all the way to the hem.

2 Either hand- or **machine-baste** the stitching line that closes the kick pleat.

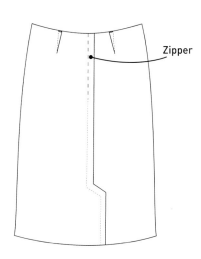

C Stitching the CB seam.

Baste a zipper in with just enough security so that you can easily run the piece under the machine without the zipper slipping off-center as you sew and turn the work. I tend to keep a needle threaded with a silk or cotton basting thread on hand so that basting is quick and no-fuss. Based on the other time-saving tips I offer, you may be surprised that I wouldn't skip this step. I've found that not taking the time to baste can really cost time if the zipper shifts when you're sewing. If you get into the habit of basting the zipper with a nice, slippery silk thread, it's actually faster.

Once you've pressed the zipper seam open, center your zipper from the back side. The position of the zipper from top to bottom on the seam is essential as well. Make sure you take into account the seam allowance of your waistband and position the zipper so that the stop will end just below the waistband. You don't want a gap between the stop and the waistband, nor do you want to sew over the zipper when applying the waistband.

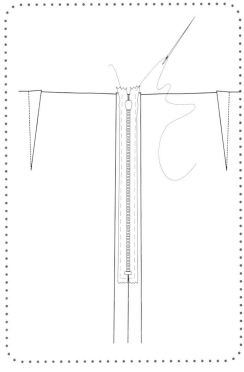

Hand-basting a zipper.

3 Press the center back seam open to the bottom of the zipper and then to the side to which the pleat falls (see **D**). Make a fold or a clip in the seam allowance to allow these areas to be pressed in different directions.

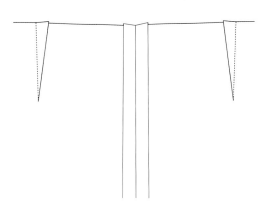

D Pressing open the center back seam.

4 Pin the zipper in place (see **E**).

5 Baste the zipper.

6 Calibrate the stitch length for your **topstitching**. Take a moment to do this, because one of the most glaring mistakes you can make is to have your most obvious stitches be too short or too long. Find a length that looks nice and doesn't distort the garment. (I even save these little samples, noting the setting on the machine so that I can go back to it quickly.) Once you've done this you can change to your zipper foot and begin your topstitching (see **F**).

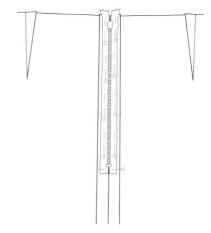

E The zipper pinned in place.

STITCHING THE SIDE SEAMS

Always sew from top to bottom or from bottom to top on an entire piece whenever you're sewing any garment with long seams. This technique keeps the finished garment from looking twisted. Be sure to press all the seams open.

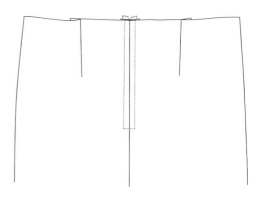

F Topstitching the zipper.

FITTING THE SKIRT

This is a great stage to do a fitting, because if you need to make any adjustments you can take care of them before you apply the waistband and finish the hem. Fit the skirt and pin out any excess fabric or note any tight areas. Take the skirt off, turn it inside out, and mark the placement of the pins with wax or chalk. Remove the pins and then redraw your new stitching lines. Don't remove the old ones. Make your corrections by sewing the new line beginning and ending about 1½ inches past the new marks so the line of stitches is doubled at the points where you're going to remove the old thread.

The finished zipper.

FINISHING

Press the seams once again and then finish their edges. You can use an **overlock** machine or serger, if you have one. I like to use pinking shears, which give a nice edge that won't unravel or add any weight or bulk to the garment—and takes a fraction of the time to do!

STEP 5: Apply the Waistband

The skirt is now ready for the waistband. You can make your waistband using a couple of different techniques, but in this project I used a traditional fabric waistband (for waistband alternatives see all the skirt variations at the end of this chapter).

1 Take the cut fabric waistband and apply fusible interfacing to it. I used a knit tricot fusible that comes in white, black, and off-white. You'll see this fusible interfacing inside many commercially made garments. I like it because you can use it with a range of fabric weights, and it's extremely flexible and durable. Use the manufacturer's recommended heat settings to apply the interfacing. Although it's recommended that you trim away seam allowances so that they do not add bulk to your finished project when using lots of interfacing, some are so lightweight you won't need to. You can quickly fuse multiple pieces for your entire project at the same time and then cut them apart and trim the excess, which will save a lot of time over the course of a project.

2 Apply the waistband to the inside of the skirt, taking into account the seam allowances on each end and the overlap for the closure.

3 After attaching the waistband, trim the excess seam allowance that will be facing the exterior of the skirt when finished. Press the seam allowances up and toward the top of the waistband.

4 Now press the bottom edge of the waistband up, so when you sew both edges together you'll get a clean finish on the bottom edge that's ready to stitch down.

5 Press the seams open and trim. After you press from this side, turn the piece and press from the right side, steaming the shape as you go.

6 At this point you can either slipstitch the bottom edge of the interior waistband down or baste and then topstitch from the exterior and "stitch in the ditch," which means topstitching very carefully while making sure the stitches fall into the seam where the waistband meets the skirt with a stitching line that is virtually invisible (see A).

7 After sewing the waistband to the skirt, take the unsewn edge of the waistband and turn it down ½ inch and press (see B). Then fold the entire waistband in half and press with right sides together. Both ends should be folded away from the skirt (see C). Sew the ends and then trim and flip the waistband right side out (see D). The inside bottom edge of the waistband can be sewn down by hand with a slipstitch. When finished, add a closure. I used a bar and hook.

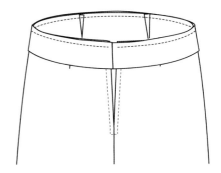

A Stitching the waistband to the skirt with right sides together.

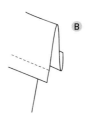

B Turn down the unsewn edge ½ inch and press. C Fold both ends away from the skirt and press with right sides together. D Sew the ends and trim, turn waistband right side out and finish inside bottom edge.

STEP 6: Hem the Skirt

The final step is to hem the skirt, for which there are a few options. On this project we will use a traditional finish, which can be done in a couple of ways. The edges can be either overlocked or pinked, or you could use seam tape. Hug-Snug is my favorite. It's a rayon tape that comes in a wide variety of colors and can be found in tailor supply shops in larger urban areas or by searching online for tailor suppliers (see Resources on page 164).

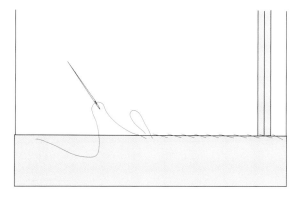

You can sew the hem up by hand using a blindstitch, whipstitch, or cross-stitch. Use a single thread and catch as few of the outer fabric threads as you can to get a beautiful, invisible hem.

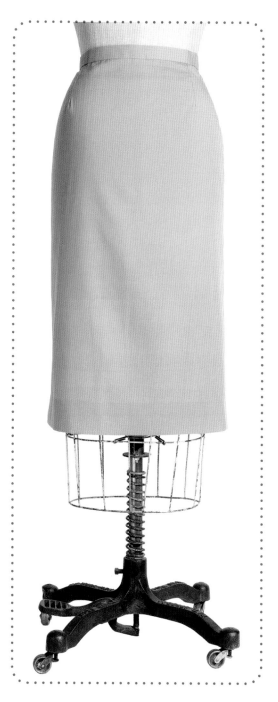

The finished skirt.

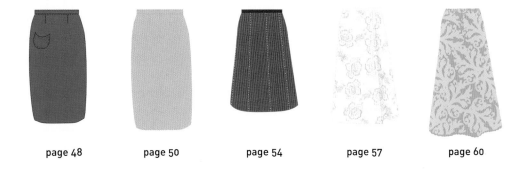

page 48　　page 50　　page 54　　page 57　　page 60

By slightly altering the
source skirt pattern,
you can create many
variations like these
above.

SKIRT VARIATIONS

Now that you've mastered the paper rub-off method, here are some
variations you can apply to pattern and sew different skirts. The fabric you
choose will determine the fullness of the finished skirt. For straight skirts
you'll want a heavier weight of fabric with less fluidity. For the two straight
skirts (see pages 48 and 50), I chose a lightweight denim and a medium-
weight woven wool. As the shape of the skirt gets fuller, you'll need softer
fabrics with a drapey feel, which will give the finished skirt more movement.
The medium-weight wool of the striped A-line skirt on page 54 is soft
enough to be fluid, but has enough body to stand away from the body nicely,
accentuating its A-line shape. For the two fuller skirts on pages 57 and 60, I
chose light- to medium-weight cotton prints.

A denim variation of the source skirt, about 3 inches shorter, features the curved patch pocket that I eliminated earlier in the step-by-step rub-off demonstration.

Casual Denim Skirt

This denim skirt is a casual interpretation of the gray wool source skirt. I added the sweet kitty cat pocket, but punched it up with some red topstitching. The kick pleat at the center back allows the skirt to be fitted nicely and still be wearable. The pockets are an exact rub-off from the gray source skirt. The pocket was traced with pins into paper and then cut out of two pieces of denim. Note that the pocket is sewn to the front of the skirt before the rest of the skirt is put together, making it easier to attach.

ADDING A POCKET

1 Pin the two pocket pieces with right sides together and stitch around the edges, leaving an opening in order to flip the pocket right side out (see **A**).

2 Next, pin the pieces and sew, leaving an opening along the top edge for the whole pocket to be turned right side out after pressing and clipping.

3 After you turn the pocket you can use a point turner to make sure the points are shaped nicely. Then give it a gentle press from the wrong side and stitch the opening closed by hand using a slipstitch (see **B**).

4 Now that you have a well-shaped pocket you're happy with, you can topstitch all around the edges with a contrasting thread color. Apply the pocket to the skirt by pinning and then sewing it by hand (see **C**).

5 The thread color is reinforced as a design choice by using the same color for a topstitching on the finished waistband.

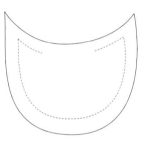

A Stitch around the edges.

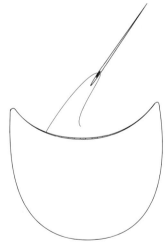

B Sewing the opening by hand with a **slipstitch**.

C The waistband and pocket are topstitched with contrasting thread.

Wool Tweed Pencil Skirt

Classic shapes in luscious fabrics never go out of style. A piece like this camel wool pencil skirt is timeless. The Petersham waistband lends a smoother line to the waistband than the wool of the skirt, and the choice of hand finishing the lapped zipper makes it blend smoothly as well. The handwork takes a little longer, but the smooth finish is well worth it.

ADDING A PETERSHAM WAISTBAND

If you're going for a quicker or less bulky look—or even a more deconstructed one—you can apply Petersham ribbon to one or both sides of the top edge of the waistband. If you use one layer, pink the top edge to avoid fraying, leaving the pinked edge to the inside for a more polished look, or place the pinked edge to the outside for a more interesting deconstructed appearance. For this skirt, I wanted a clean and polished finish, so I sandwiched the skirt's top seam allowance between two pieces of the Petersham ribbon and topstitched all around.

ADDING A KICK PLEAT

The kick pleat is modified into a simple slit by turning back both sides of the pleat and mitering the corner that forms at the hem. The stitching at the top of the slit is reinforced with only the bar from a skirt hook set. This is a clever and common trick used in high-end women's wear, as it adds longevity to a garment.

A Petersham waistband is less bulky than a traditional fabric waistband made from the same wool as the skirt.

The source skirt kick pleat is converted into a simple slit.

This variation of the source skirt is knee length with a Petersham ribbon waistband and center back slit at the hem.

If you'd like to give your finished garment a beautiful couture look, or if you're working with a fabric like crepe or velvet that's very spongy and doesn't like topstitching, put in the zipper by hand.

Start by doubling your thread. To keep it from tangling or forming knots, you can apply beeswax, or use this little tip I learned from Isis Mussenden, costume designer for *The Chronicles of Narnia: The Lion, the Witch, and the Wardrobe* and *Prince Caspian*: Put both ends of the thread through the eye of the needle, then feed them back through the loop at the end. Pull the threads taut so that there's a little knot just behind the eye of the needle. You might think that this would keep the thread from going through the fabric, but because it's the same size as the needle it goes right through. I have no idea why this works so well—it must have something to do with keeping both threads the same length—but it essentially keeps your thread from knotting as you do the handwork.

1 Begin at the top of one side of the zipper and pull the thread through to the top side, making a little **backstitch** and moving down about ¼ to ⅜ inch per stitch, backstitching all the way around.

2 Unzip the zipper and machine-stitch the right side to the seam allowance of the skirt opening with right sides together, close to the zipper teeth. Then press the skirt fabric away from the zipper.

3 Press and align the seam, then, by hand, use tiny backstitches to topstitch the zipper all around at about ⅜ of an inch apart for a nearly invisible finish.

A lapped zipper.

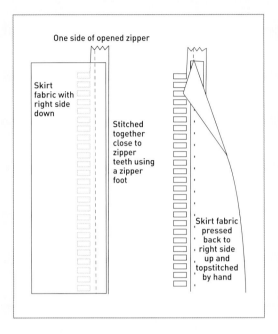

One side of opened zipper

Skirt fabric with right side down

Stitched together close to zipper teeth using a zipper foot

Skirt fabric pressed back to right side up and topstitched by hand

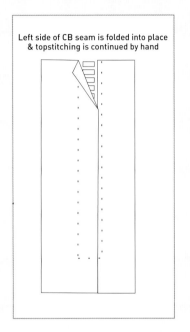

Left side of CB seam is folded into place & topstitching is continued by hand

After stitching the first side by machine, press the skirt away so the teeth are unimpeded. Using a tiny backstitch, topstitch this side of the zipper by hand.

Align the opposite side of the skirt seam over the teeth of the zipper, making sure the top edges of the skirt match at the top and pin in place. Continue your hand backstitching all the way around.

For a smooth hand-stitch that doesn't knot, put both ends of the thread through the eye of the needle and then through the loop to ensure that they remain the same length. Knot the ends as you normally would and sew. The "knot" created is the same size as the needle, so it passes through the fabric while keeping the thread from tangling.

Striped A-Line Skirt

Converting the sloper for your straight skirt to an A-line is easy and gives you many styling options. This variation is a basic A-line skirt in red wool with texture and interest. Also included are instructions for matching up stripes to create a **chevron** pattern at the side seams.

If you need to alter the size or shape, sometimes it's good to save the original pattern and trace onto another sheet of paper using your needle wheel. This way you can manipulate the pattern, but still have the straight skirt to use later. The idea here is to pivot the dart closed and take in the side seams to fit the waist, pivoting out the bottom of the side seam at the same time.

CONVERTING THE SOURCE PATTERN INTO AN A-LINE

1 Make a line down the middle of the skirt pattern piece through the dart (or darts) and cut the pattern in half (see **A**).

2 Close up the dart and swing out the bottom of the side seams from the hip and down to the hem.

3 Align the two sides of the dart to close the dart as if it were sewn (see **B**). This makes the bottom of the skirt open up. Tape the dart closed and then tape the modified pattern to another sheet of kraft paper.

4 Straighten out any curve along the side in the hip area, as it will no longer be needed in this version. The idea is to get a smooth flare from the waist to the hem: a typical A-line.

5 Do the same with the back piece.

A Petersham waistband makes the waistband less bulky. Like the Wool Tweed Pencil Skirt on page 50, it encloses the top edge of the skirt.

A Draw a line down the middle of the pattern piece and through the dart.

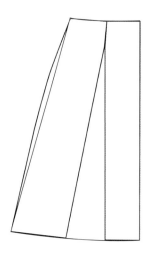

B Spread the bottom of the skirt from the dart.

Our source pattern is converted into an A-line pattern in a striped red wool fabric, finished with a Petersham waistband.

One of the most obvious differences between custom-made and mass-manufactured clothing is the matching of stripes and patterns. It takes longer to do, but it makes the finished garment much more desirable to wear.

The first thing you must know is that you'll need to cut each piece individually to make sure all the stripes will line up exactly along the seam lines when you sew the garment together. Begin with the center front piece and lay it out so the fold lies on an area of the fabric that will make a pleasing line up the front of the skirt.

After placing the first piece, mark where the stripes meet at the seam line *before* cutting out the fabric. Do this by laying a ruler along the stripe and continuing the line onto the paper pattern as shown at right. Notice in the illustration that the **fold line** is placed directly between two stripes so the pattern on the front of the skirt will be balanced on both sides.

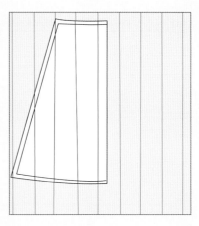

Lay out the pattern on the striped fabric and then mark the lines before you cut so you'll have a visual reference when cutting the subsequent pieces.

ALIGNING STRIPES

Working on the next adjoining piece and then around the skirt, fold the seam line back on your nonstriped paper pattern and match up the seam lines with the marked piece where they will be sewn. Now you'll be able to see where the stripes will intersect at the seam (see box above). Make a clear mark at the point where they intersect and then take the newly marked piece to the fabric and align the paper pattern on the fabric so that the stripes will fall on the points you just marked (see **C**). You're limited by the grain line of the fabric, so don't let matching a stripe exactly throw off your grain line. The most important factor is for the stripes to intersect at the same points.

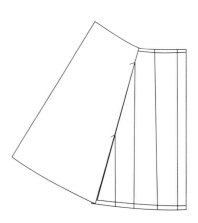

C Folding the seam allowance back on the next piece and lining up the top and bottom as if they were sewn.

Reversible Cotton Wrap Skirt

Once you have a basic A-line shape (see page 54), take the back and two skirt front patterns to create this cute wrap skirt. Can't decide which fabric to use from your collection? Pick two coordinating fabrics and make one reversible skirt. It's easy. Just cut out one skirt of each fabric and then sew them together. Polish it off by sandwiching the top edge in Petersham or ribbon and then topstitching. Make the ties long enough to wrap around, or you can apply a skirt hook to close.

CREATING A WRAP SKIRT

1 Cut two A-line skirt front pieces and one A-line skirt back piece from the Striped A-line Skirt pattern (see page 54) and make two skirts. You may want to cut out a couple of inches from the skirt front pattern for less overlap. I cut off 3 inches for this example (see **A**).

2 Sew the right sides together around the hem, leaving the waist open (see **B**).

This skirt is reversible.

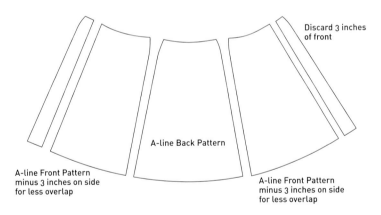

Discard 3 inches of front

A-line Back Pattern

A-line Front Pattern minus 3 inches on side for less overlap

A-line Front Pattern minus 3 inches on side for less overlap

A Two A-line skirt front patterns and one skirt back pattern create the wrap skirt.

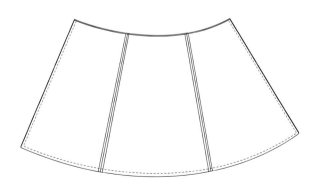

B Sewing the two skirts together around the edges.

3 Start with the first side and wrap the raw edge of the ribbon around the skirt waist seam. Then pin all the way across the waist seam to the other side and let the excess be loose for your tie. Now take the other piece and fold the raw end of the ribbon over ½ inch and pin it over the area where the first ribbon came off the end of the waist. Pin this side all the way around the waist of the skirt and let the end hang off. Both raw edges should be tucked inside the "waistband" and there should be two ties that hang off both ends.

4 Apply Petersham ribbon to the waist. Measure the full length of the waist measurement and then add enough to go around the waist as well as to tie a bow—the measurement will differ depending on your waist measurements and how long you'd like the bow to be.

5 Sandwich the raw edge of the waist between the two lengths of ribbon (see C).

6 Secure the waistband by topstitching all around, about ⅛ inch from the edge (see D).

7 Make a buttonhole on one of the side seams at the waistband to wrap one end neatly around the other.

The ribbon-tie waist closure.

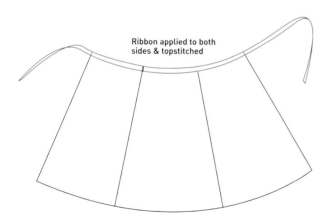

Ribbon applied to both sides & topstitched

C The top edge of the skirt is enclosed in ribbon so the raw edges are clean finished, and the ribbon can be extended as far as you like to make ties that either knot or bow.

D The waistband with topstitching.

Two skirts created by using three panels from the Striped A-line Skirt variation (see page 54) are sewn together to create this comfortable, reversible wrap skirt with a ribbon-tie waist closure.

Cotton Bias-Cut Skirt

This super-simple bias-cut A-line skirt is a lovely way to feature a bold fabric print. The bias cut makes the shape even softer and more relaxed, and allows for a fast wave-cut hem, which in this example I've punctuated with a layer of wave-cut bias tape. If you prefer a deconstructed look, you could leave the edges of the bias hem raw, pinked, or overlocked. The practical pockets and drawstring waistband make this a summer weekend wardrobe staple.

ALTERING THE A-LINE PATTERN

Take the A-line skirt pattern from the Striped A-line Skirt (see page 54). Extend the sides to elongate the entire skirt. (I extended it by 18 inches for this example.) To have a better drape, rotate the pattern 45° and cut the skirt on the bias.

The pockets are hidden in the side seams.

MAKING THE POCKETS

1 Begin by tracing the corner of your skirt pattern onto a sheet of kraft paper.

2 To mark the shape of the pocket, measure the area at the corner of the skirt that your wrist and spread fingertips take up. Mark the rough, rounded shape onto the pattern (see **A**).

3 Use a curve tool to smooth the curve on the side opposite the seam allowance (see **B**). This is your pocket pattern.

Corner of skirt

A Measuring the corner of the skirt.

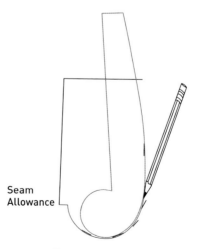

Seam Allowance

B Making the pocket shape.

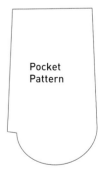

Pocket Pattern

This skirt variation is an elongated an A-line skirt pattern that features two pockets on the side and a wave-cut hem. In addition, due to being cut on the bias, it has a relaxed, flowing look.

4 Cut out four of these pocket shapes. Apply each of the four pocket pieces to a corner of the skirt at the upper side seams, where pockets are usually found.

5 Pin and sew the pockets to the skirt front and back separately (see **C**).

6 Trim the seams and press them toward the pocket (see **D**).

7 Now with both the skirt front and back having pocket pieces extending from their sides, sew the skirt and pockets together along the side seams and around the pocket and then at the top of the side seams to close up the skirt sides, leaving an opening to put your hands in the pockets (see **E**).

8 Turn down the raw edge at the top of the waistband and then turn down again and press (see **F**). Open the turned-down waistband up again and mark the center point on what will be the front at a place that will be covered when the waistband is turned back down again. Make a buttonhole at the mark for the drawstring.

9 Turn the waistband down again, press, and topstitch to make the casing. Illustration **G** shows the waistband from the inside of the front. The folded-down waistband finishes the tops of the pockets. Add a soft ribbon tie by attaching a safety pin to one end of the ribbon and threading it through the casing.

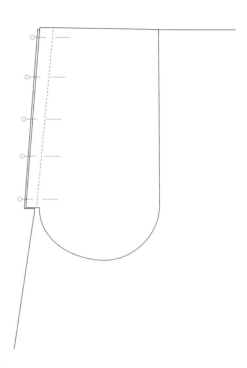

C Pinning the pocket pieces at the side seams.

CREATING THE HEM

1 To make the hem, cut the edge of the skirt with wave pinking shears.

2 Apply contrasting bias strip and then cut it with wave pinking shears.

A self-waistband.

A wave-cut bias hem.

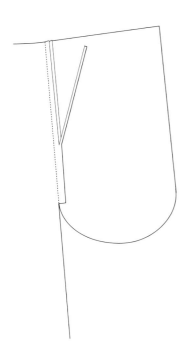

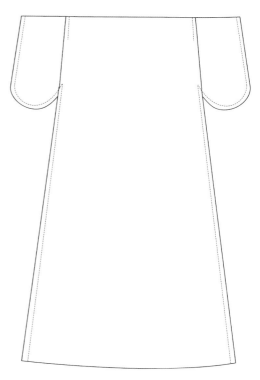

D Pressing the pockets away from the skirt and trimming the seam allowances.

E Sewing the skirt together at the side seams around the pockets.

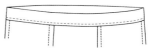

F The top raw edge turned down and buttonhole placed in the center to insert the drawstring.

G The top edge of the skirt is folded down again, leaving about ¾ inch.

CHAPTER 3

PATTERNING
DRESSES

THE SOURCE DRESS

Our source dress for this rub-off project is a vintage 1960s sheath. It has a front and two back pieces with a zipper in the center back. The bodice is shaped by two bust darts on each side. There are two kick pleats at each side seam. It has short sleeves and the neckline has a facing.

The dress opens from the back with a lapped zipper.

The vintage 1960s source sheath dress.

The dress has kick pleats at the side seams, each accented with a bow.

The Fabric Rub-Off Method

Unlike the paper rub-off method in which we pin directly into kraft paper and then trace the pin holes to create a pattern, the fabric rub-off method begins by draping fabric over the source garment and then tracing the seams and pattern directly onto the fabric. Although muslin is the most common tracing fabric to use, I used Do-Sew for this project so that my tracing would appear more clearly in the step-by-step photographs. The tracing fabric then serves as the pattern. As we'll see, sometimes transferring the fabric pattern onto kraft paper is needed, especially when altering the measurements of the source garment. Once the pattern is created, altered, and cut out, we're off to the sewing stage.

I will use our vintage source dress to demonstrate how to pattern using the fabric rub-off, which, as we learned in Chapter 1, is great to use when the source garment contains more complex style features like pleats or for three-dimensional objects, such as purses. In addition, it's a great method to use when you don't want to pin directly into the source garment, as weights can be used to hold and keep the garment and fabric in place. I used pins instead of weights in this project because it's easier to see the seam lines in the demonstration photos. However, if you have a garment that won't withstand pinning, you can just as easily use pattern weights.

The neckline is finished with a facing inside.

We begin the fabric rub-off technique by first tracing the source dress.

BODICE FRONT

1 Begin by laying out the dress. Fold the front of the dress in half and pin or weight it to itself to keep it in place.

2 Using a pencil or invisible marker, draw a vertical line onto the tracing fabric along the straight of grain to represent the bodice's center front fold line. Then draw a perpendicular line off the bottom of the center front fold line to make an L shape, as was done for the skirt in Chapter 2. This line will represent the waistline.

3 Lay the tracing fabric over the dress.

4 Align and pin the bodice's center front fold along the CF pencil line on the fabric. Then align and pin the waistline to the perpendicular pencil line on the fabric. Notice how the dress doesn't fit perfectly into the L shape. Don't force the dress to fit in it. Any deviations from the L shape will be noted later and will give us clues on how to shape the dress (see **A**).

5 Smooth the tracing fabric to the outer edges of the bodice and pin all along the perimeter without moving the dress (see **B**).

6 Keeping the tracing fabric flat against the bodice, begin smoothing it around the armhole and neckline. Pin the seam lines as you go (see **C**).

7 After you've pinned all around the perimeter of the bodice front, fold the sleeve back to check and see that you've pinned the bodice's edges correctly (see **D**).

8 With a pencil or marker, lightly trace all of the seam lines and darts. Use your straightedge and curve tools to help. Make any notes you'll need for the sewing stage, such as junctures and darts (see **E**).

9 Measure the darts from the inside of the bodice to find how much fabric you'll need for the darts. Recreate the darts on the pattern using the dart lines from the tracing as one side and making the other leg of each dart to match the measurements. To add in this amount to the edges of the pattern, find the area along the center front line that has been pulled off center from the shaping of the darts. Subtract this amount and divide the difference between the seams on either side of the darts. Any additional amount will be added into the other edges. Make sure the measurements add up to the total amount of the darts (see **F**).

A Pinning the tracing fabric along the bodice's center front fold and waistline.

B Pinning the bottom edges of the bodice front. Notice the delineation of the dart placement.

C Pinning along the neckline, shoulder seams, and armhole.

D The entire bodice front pinned all around.

BODICE BACK

1 Begin rubbing off the bodice back by folding the back of the dress along the center back seam and pinning it to itself.

2 Draw an L on a new piece of tracing fabric, as we did in Step 2 for the bodice front (see page 68).

3 Cover the bodice back with a new piece of tracing fabric.

4 Align and pin the center back seam along the vertical pencil line on the tracing fabric. Then align and pin the waistline to the horizontal pencil line on the tracing fabric (see G).

5 Follow Steps 5–9 of the bodice front (see page 68) to pin and trace the bodice back.

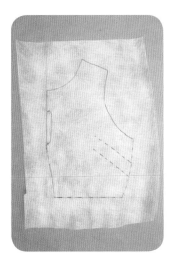

E The lines of the pattern traced in.

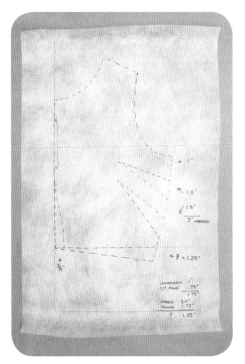

F Measuring the darts and adding the same amount to the outer edges.

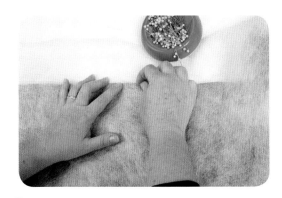

G Pinning the tracing fabric along the bodice back's center back seam.

SLEEVES

1 To trace the sleeves, begin by folding a sleeve in half, making sure the underarm seam is flat and smooth. Most set-in sleeves, such as this one, will not be symmetrical on either side of the fold line; therefore, you need to draw the center line on the tracing fabric and then place the line on the sleeve fold with enough room to flip the sleeve and trace the other side. Match the line and fold.

2 Trace the armhole, the underarm seam, and the sleeve hem. At this stage notice how the line you drew for the fold does not match the actual fold of the sleeve. The folded edge of the sleeve will pull away from the line toward the top edge. This is the amount of fabric that creates the ease in the top of the sleeve.

3 Look at the shape of the top edge of the sleeve. There should be a noticeable fullness that begins midway up the armhole. Make a mark on the tracing fabric, which will serve as the sleeve notch. This is where you'll ease the extra fabric from the sleeve cap into the armhole of the sleeve when you're sewing (see H).

4 Being careful to maintain the same fold line on your sleeve, turn the sleeve to the other side and replace the tracing, continuing to smooth, pin or weight, and trace (see I).

5 Make the same notation on this side of where the ease begins.

6 Remove the tracing pieces and see if the outer top edge is symmetrical. There will typically be a shallow curve to the front of the sleeve. This is very important to ensure a good fit, as our arms move forward. The only exception to this case is when you might need more of a curve, such as a dance costume that requires a lot of movement. However, for a standard set-in sleeve the finished piece will fit and look better if there is more of a curve to the back and less to the front. Author Kathleen Fasanella provides a wonderful explanation of this concept in her book *The Entrepreneur's Guide to Sewn Product Manufacturing*.

SKIRT

Trace the skirt pieces using the same steps discussed in Chapter 2 starting on page 30.

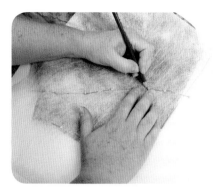

H Tracing the front half of the sleeve onto the tracing fabric piece, marking the center line, and applying notches to denote the front and back.

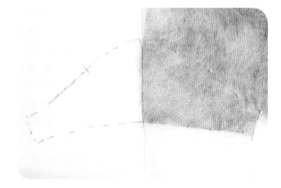

I Aligning the folded sleeve to the tracing fabric along the folded line to begin tracing the other side.

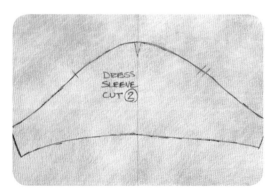

J Fabric pattern labeled with front and back notations and shoulder seam mark.

STEP 2: Create the Dress and Facing Patterns

Now that all the pieces have been traced onto the tracing fabric, we will use the information we recorded and begin to create the dress pattern.

1 Draw all of the seam lines with a straight edge. Use the curve tool to create the armhole and neckline curves (see **A**).

2 Make notations of the garment and cutting instructions, such as fold lines, notches, ease, and hemlines.

ALTERING THE DRESS PATTERN

If you need to make adjustments to the size or style of the dress, this is the stage to do it. The same methods we used to alter the skirt in Chapter 2 (see page 35) can be applied; however, with the bodice you'll want to make the slash-and-spread lines (see pages 110–111) in a specific place. In this project I'll increase the bodice's measurements to fit a larger size.

We could add more measurements to the center, but that would increase the neckline and make the neck opening look sloppy. In addition, we don't want to increase the shoulder seam because a larger person's shoulder isn't necessarily larger. Instead, make slash-and-spread marks and then determine how much you need to add by taking the bust and waist measurements of the wearer and the measurement of the bust on the pattern as is. Our source dress bust measures 30 inches and we'd like it to fit a person with a bust of 32 inches. We know the difference is 2 inches, but remember, we need ease so the dress doesn't look upholstered to the person. Starting with 2 inches of ease will give us a total of 4 inches to add. By dividing the 4 inches among the four sections that comprise the entire bodice will mean we will add 1 inch to each section. Do the same for the waist. Based on our measurements we will add 1 inch at the bust and 1 and 1 1/2 inches at the waist. After you cut the pattern, spread it out onto another piece of tracing fabric or kraft paper (this will retain the source garment's original measurements) and mark all of the edges. We now have our new, altered bodice. Repeat the process with the skirt pattern, referring to the alteration methods for determining the fullness of the skirt in Chapter 2 (see page 38).

This is also the stage where you can add or subtract to the waist seam. You can remove a waist seam by aligning the darts on the skirt's bodice and front and taping the pieces together to make one continuous dress front and back.

To make the sleeve pattern smaller, you can fold out the excess as shown in illustration **B** with the sleeve pattern.

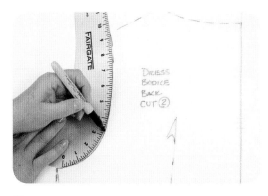

A Tracing the outer edges with a straight edge and curve tool.

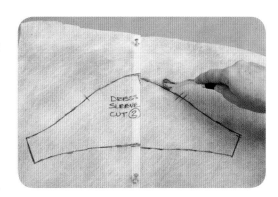

B Tracing the reduced sleeve onto another piece of kraft paper to make a smaller version.

To make the sleeve pattern larger, you can slash and spread it as in other sections. Trace the sleeve pattern onto another sheet of kraft paper to create the altered size sleeve pattern if you'd like to maintain the original rub-off pattern (see C).

CREATING FACING AND INTERFACING PATTERNS

Facing is used to finish the rough edges of a garment. Typical areas include necklines, open sleeves, and hems. Facing gives a clean, finished-looking line. Since a facing will fit the finished edge, it should be made before seam allowances. Facing is cut as the same shape of an edge, so we will simply use our revised bodice pattern to create our facing pattern.

Interfacing gives stability and body to a garment; it can also stiffen a piece. Usually, interfacing reinforces a facing. The most common types of interfacing are fusible (also called iron-on) and sew-on. For our project we will use a sew-on interfacing to line our facing and will therefore need to create a pattern for it. Note that we'll be cutting the facing pattern twice: one for the interfacing and one for the fabric.

1 Take the revised bodice pattern and measure 2 inches below and around the neckline (see D).

2 Finish the curve of the facing pattern with a curve tool.

3 Place the facing pattern on a new sheet of kraft paper. Use a tracing wheel to trace around the facing (see E).

4 Lift off the bodice pattern and draw in the lines you've transferred using a pencil, straight edge, and curve tool as needed.

5 Mark the grain line and note any cutting instructions on the facing pattern. The grain line should match the bodice pattern. In this case, the center front and the center back are one on the straight of grain.

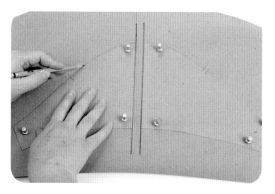

C Altering the sleeve by slashing and spreading it.

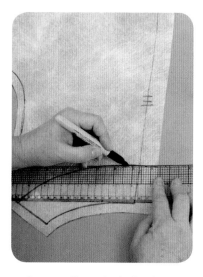

D Use a ruler to easily mark 2 inches below and around the neckline to create the facing pattern.

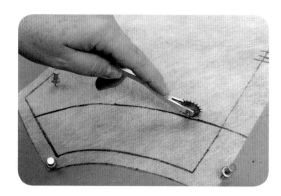

E Use a tracing wheel to trace the facing onto kraft paper.

I once had to rub off a dress overnight for the TV show *3rd Rock from the Sun*. We were shooting a special episode that was supposed to be spectacular. The script called for a dream/fantasy sequence for each of the main characters, so that meant a lot of additional costumes.

Melina Root, the costume designer, gave me a vintage dress to duplicate for Kristin Johnston to wear in a dancing scene for the next day. Well, I was in such a hurry that I forgot a few rules that I now always follow because of this experience. First, I was rubbing off a garment that was a vintage rayon crepe fabric. However, the new garment was supposed to be made of silk charmeuse. The original had significant give and stretch to it. The new fabric, though similar in drape, had far less give. This alone should have caused me to add a bit more ease into the pattern . . . but I didn't. Next, I should have been more careful to pull the original taut to maintain the full size of the original, but I was in a hurry and I didn't. Lastly, I should have added ample seam allowance in the side seams to allow for any mistakes in my calculations, but, of course, I didn't.

So I made the dress and we arrived on set the next day, and it fit as if it had been put in the dryer and shrunk. Yikes! I quickly swooped it away and let out every possible seam there was to let out as much as I could. I vowed then that I would never use such scant seam allowances.

ADDING SEAM ALLOWANCES

Now that we have all our pieces altered we're ready to add seam allowances around the perimeter of all the pattern pieces, with the exception of those pieces to be placed on the fold like the bodice front, the skirt front, and the sleeve. Refer to "Adding Seam Allowances" in Chapter 2 (see page 39) to determine the amount of seam allowance you'd like to add. For this dress you may want to give a little extra in the center back seam or the side seams.

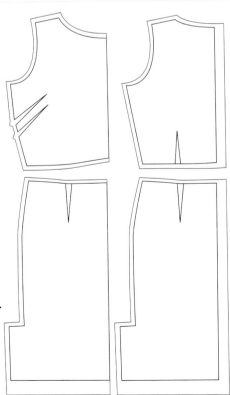

F Adding seam allowance to the dress pattern.

STEP 3: Cut the Fabric

We are now ready to cut out the dress fabric from our patterns.

1 Lay out the fabric with the dress pattern on top and in the proper grain direction (see **A**). Take into account any prints your fabric may have and make sure the placement of any large graphic elements are going to end up in a flattering arrangement (see page 56). Depending on the pattern, for example, you wouldn't want to have two large flowers directly over the breasts—or maybe you would, depending on the context! (I can think of a few costume ideas where this would be very funny.) The old adage holds true: Measure twice, cut once. You only get one chance to cut, so check all these things before you do.

2 Once you have all the pattern pieces arranged, use fabric weights, or pins, to anchor the pieces.

3 Cut out all the pieces, noting any notches as you go.

4 Use tracing paper and a tracing wheel to mark your darts and notches. Fold the tracing paper in half, insert it between the two pieces of fabric you've just cut, and then trace with the wheel, making sure you're marking on the wrong side of the fabric.

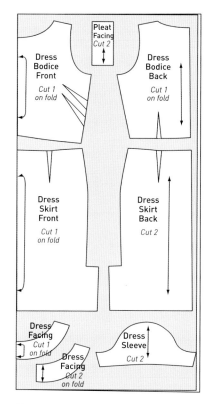

A Laying out the dress pattern so that all the patterns' grain lines run parallel to the selvage edge.

QUICK CUTTING WITHOUT PINS

Here's another little "down and dirty" secret I'd like to share with you. If I have a fabric rub-off that I've made and the hand, or tactile feel, of the fabric I'm using grabs the tracing fabric and doesn't shift around on the fabric, I won't use pins or weights. I just hold the edges of the fabric piece I'm cutting as I go. If this makes you uneasy and you feel as if the result will turn out sloppy, then by all means use weights or pins. However, if you try it and it works for you, then here is yet another sort of guerrilla sewing tactic that has given me great freedom and productivity. Again, if for any reason this affects the quality of your work, then back up and try something else. I just find that when I'm in a crunch and find a way to cut a corner it's just the right push to find a whole new approach.

The sewing process of the dress is similar to the sewing for other projects in that you should begin by sewing the smaller areas that need to be sewn first, while they remain flat. Remember, we cut a garment from large pieces to small pieces, but we sew from small to large. This allows you to batch the similar tasks and saves time and effort, making the whole process go more smoothly.

DARTS, STAYSTITCHING, AND EASESTITCHING

Take all pieces that require darts and stitch them all at the same sitting. For this dress, there are two darts on each side of the bodice front, one on the bodice back, two on the skirt front, and one on each skirt back.

1 Using your marks from the tracing paper, pin the darts and sew them as you did on the skirt in Chapter 2 (see page 42).

2 Before moving on to pressing, stitch all areas that need **staystitching** or easestitching (see **A**). In this case the neckline of the bodice front and back and the armholes need to be staystitched just outside the stitching line. This keeps the neckline from stretching as you handle it while you sew, and makes a nicer finished neckline that doesn't gap out and away from the body. (This is a great trick if you have a ready-made garment with a gaping neckline. You can adjust it back into shape either by machine- or hand-stitching to snug it back into place.)

3 While you're still sitting, make an easestitch at the top of the sleeve pieces (called the sleeve cap or sleeve head). Use a stitch length that's going to be easy to gather when pulling the bobbin thread. You'll want this option later when we are setting in the sleeve (see **B**).

4 Sew the sleeve underarm seams.

PRESSING

Take all the pieces to your **pressing area** and press. Press the darts downward on the bodice pieces and press the darts toward the side seams on the skirt pieces. Use a pressing ham to shape the darts and a sleeve board to press the sleeve underarm seams open. You can either pink or overlock all the side seams at this point.

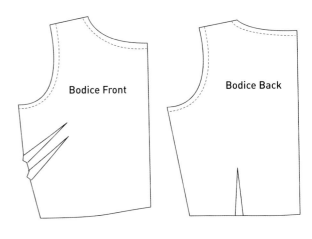

Bodice Front   Bodice Back

A Staystitching the neckline and armholes.

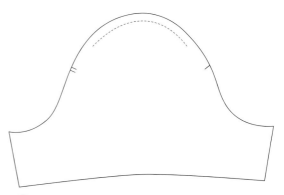

B Easestitch a single row here for setting in the sleeve cap later.

STAYSTITCHING AND EASESTITCHING

There are areas on a cut garment that are more prone to stretching because they usually fall on the bias. As mentioned in Chapter 1, fabric has more stretch on the bias. Therefore, we use additional rows of stitching to maintain the stability of a neckline or armhole, which is called staystitching. If we want to go further than just maintaining the length of the original cut line and use a line of stitching to draw the fabric in to the point of nearly gathering, but not quite, this is called easestitching. You're able to "ease" one larger-length stitching line into a slightly shorter-length stitching line, creating a bit of shape or a bit of fullness without a dart or gather. These principles are very important in taking your work from a basic beginner level to a finer, more custom-made level.

Staystitching is a very important step in keeping the neckline from stretching out as you handle the garment during sewing. Once during a sewing workshop I was teaching, I pointed out a garment that was gaping at the neckline. Oftentimes, the neckline's shape requires part of the seam to be on the bias, which allows for stretching. Staystitching all openings, such as necks and armholes, keeps the stitching line from stretching because even though the fabric stretches, the stitching line doesn't, therefore stabilizing the edge and maintaining the shape of the original pattern piece. This saves time in the long run because if the neckline stretches during sewing, you'll have to alter the garment to adjust for it later. These are the things that'll make everything go smoother later, if you just take the time to do them now. I like to save time on areas that don't really matter in the final fit of the garment, like using a rotary cutter or using pinking shears instead of adding bulk and threading time with my overlock machine when I think it won't matter in the fit or the look of the final garment.

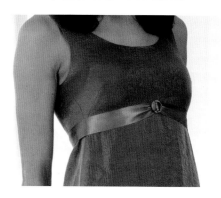

The fluidity of this dress variation's fabric (see page 90) needed staystitching to shape the smooth lines in the neck and arms.

Sometimes when you're cutting a pattern that someone else will be sewing, you'll need to mark all the cutting lines for him or her so that there's a high degree of accuracy. Unfortunately, this takes an extraordinary amount of time, so if you're not marking your seam lines and don't have a stitching line to follow, you can use the outer edge of the fabric against the line on your sewing machine as a guide to how large the seam allowances will be. If you put the piece through the overlock machine before you sew the seams, you can easily trim away anywhere from 0–¼ inch, depending on your accuracy. This, in effect, moves your stitching line in by that amount and can make the finished garment smaller in those areas. Why can't I account for this and take ⅛ inch off and overlock or pink before I sew? Because some seams need to be graded, meaning one side (the side closest to the outside when pressed) will be trimmed a bit shorter.

The final dress variation with staystitching.

77

ASSEMBLING THE DRESS BACK

We now have to **assemble** the dress front and back. We'll begin with the dress back.

1 Pin each of the bodice back pieces to its corresponding skirt back piece and sew each at the waist seams.

2 Leaving the zipper area open, apply a lapped zipper (see pages 52–53). First determine where the zipper will end and mark this spot on the center back seams.

3 Sew the center back seam, beginning at the point where the zipper will end and then continue sewing all the way to the hem of the skirt.

4 Before pressing the center back seam open, place the dress back on the work surface in front of you with both sides facing each other and the center back seam on the right. Take the zipper face up and insert it between the two pieces, aligning the top edge where you would like the zipper to stop and accounting for the facing that will be applied at the neck edge. Pin the zipper to the top piece only along the edge and then fold the back piece of the dress away so that you can sew the zipper to the center back seam with a zipper foot, stitching 1/8 inch away from the zipper teeth.

5 After the first side of the zipper is sewn, press the fabric away from the zipper teeth and tuck the tail of the zipper back and behind the opening in the center back of the dress (see **C**). Then topstitch along the edge where the zipper and center back seam join, about 1/8 inch from the edge.

6 Next bring the side of the dress facing your left back up to meet the zipper, folding back the seam allowance as you go. Pin the folded edge of the dress to the zipper, making sure the folded edge covers the zipper teeth completely and meets the dress fabric on the other side of the zipper so the zipper won't be visible after it's sewn.

7 Using the zipper foot, continue from where you finished the topstitching of the first side and topstitch around the second side of the zipper back up to the neck edge (see **D**).

8 The entire dress back is now ready to go. Set it aside.

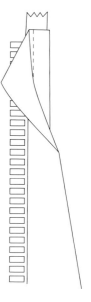

C Sewing the zipper to one side of the center back seam.

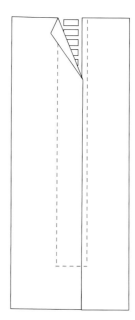

D Folding the second side of the center back seam and continuing to topstitch this side to complete the lapped zipper.

ASSEMBLING THE DRESS FRONT

Moving on to the dress front, pin the bodice front and the skirt front with right sides together.

1 Stitch the front waist seam.

2 Press the front waist seam down and toward the skirt.

3 Pink or overlock the seams, **grading** the seam toward the outside (see **E**).

CONNECTING THE DRESS BACK AND FRONT

Now it's time to connect the different sections of the dress we have worked on separately up to this point.

1 Pin the completed front and back sections together at the shoulder seams and side seams. (This stitching order makes altering the size in or out much easier.)

2 Stitch the shoulder seams together. If your fabric is super-stretchy, this is a nice place to add a piece of twill tape or Hug-Snug, as you sew to keep the shoulder seam from stretching out.

3 Press the shoulder seams open and finish the edges (see **F**).

4 Pin the side seams together and stitch.

5 Press the side seams open and finish the edges (see **G**).

E The finished dress front (bodice and skirt) assembled, with the waist seam pressed down.

F Stitching and pressing the shoulder seams open.

G Sewing and pressing the side seams.

A QUICK FITTING

This is the point where you should fit the garment. The major seams have been sewn together, but the facings and hems have not. If you want, you could also baste the sleeve for fitting so that it can be easily adjusted later.

SETTING IN THE SLEEVES

Sleeves can be the most difficult, frustrating part of sewing, but if you're patient you can quickly and easily learn how to put in a beautiful sleeve!

1 Turn the dress inside out.

2 Identify the front and back of the sleeves by the notches. This is where your measuring and marking earlier really pays off. Pin each sleeve to its proper counterpart armhole, just for sorting purposes.

3 Pin the underarm seams together, making sure you have the right sides together. There's nothing more frustrating than sewing your sleeves inside out or backwards—and let's be honest; we've all done that more than once!

4 Pin the top of the sleeve cap to the shoulder seam. This is where the mark you made earlier to show where the sleeve meets the shoulder seam mark is very helpful, as you can easily tweak the grain of the sleeve either forward or back and it can throw off the whole fit and look of the garment.

5 Pin the underarm area from side to side, making sure the pieces are smooth.

6 The sleeve is now pinned, except for the sleeve cap. This is where you'll have to do some easing. Think of the armhole as a clock face. You should pin the sleeve at the 12, 3, and 9 o'clock positions. Then place pins at the 4, 5, 6, 7, and 8 positions. When you're sure this is evenly distributed, pin evenly again at the 1 and 2, then 10 and 11 positions as shown in photo **H**.

7 At this point I like to put extra pins between all the pins between 9 and 3 o'clock positions along the top of the armhole. This is the way I pin every time, and it's the best way I know of getting a smooth, even sleeve cap. Regardless of the type of garment and fabric, if it has a set-in sleeve, I always do this.

8 The fabric should now be smoothly pinned together along the underarm and there should be a bit of ease through the sleeve cap. If there is ease through the underarm, unpin and shift it up.

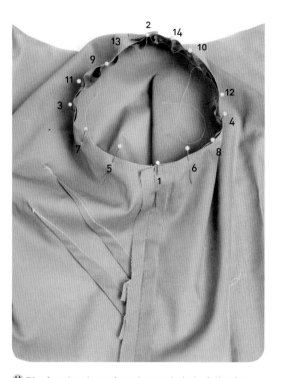

H Pinning the sleeve into the armhole by following the order in Step 6 allows for even distribution through the underarm. Ease is concentrated into the sleeve cap to help the sleeve curve nicely into the bodice.

9 This is where you'll pull the bobbin thread of the easestitching you did on page 75. This allows the very top edge of the sleeve to have a bit more fullness than just fitting into the armhole completely flat. This little bit of molding accommodates the fullness of your upper arm. Pull the bobbin thread gently until the dimension of the sleeve cap matches the dimension of the armhole.

10 If you feel confident, you can stitch the armhole and sleeve together at this point. If you'd like to test the fit, you can baste the sleeve in and then fit the sleeve.

11 Make any adjustments needed to the sleeve and stitch.

12 While the dress is still inside out, press the seam allowance toward the sleeves. I do this by placing a sleeve board inside the body and sleeve as if the sleeve board were the shoulder area and then gently pressing.

13 Repeat Steps 3–13 for the other sleeve.

FACINGS

When you're confident that the shoulder and neckline measurements are what you want, it's time to assemble the facings. Apply interfacing to the facing pieces. If there was any adjustment to the shoulder seam or neckline, make adjustments accordingly to the facings.

1 Stitch the facing pieces together.

2 Press open and finish the edges. It's a good idea to stitch and pink the edge for stability.

3 Apply the facing to the neckline by pinning the right sides together.

4 Stitch around the neckline (see **I**).

5 Remove pins and clip into the curve all the way around, about ½ inch apart (see **J**).

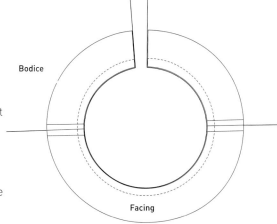

I Stitching the facing to the neckline.

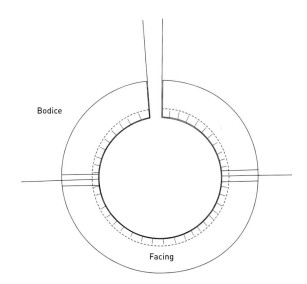

J Clipping and trimming the neckline.

6 Press the facing away from the bodice from the inside with the seam going toward the facing (see **K**).

7 Pin the seam toward the facing from the right side and then machine-stitch a line ⅛ inch from the seam on the facing side. This is what we call edgestitching (see page 76), and it keeps the facing from rolling out to the outside (see **L**).

8 Fold the facing into place. It should lie properly before you press it. If it doesn't, you'll need to give it another clip. Clip and check until you're happy with the way it lies. Trim and grade the seam.

9 Gently press from the inside, making sure to not press the facing edge, but the neckline only (see **M**).

10 Fold and shape the ends of the facings in the center back around the zipper and stitch them by hand using a blindstitch (see **N**).

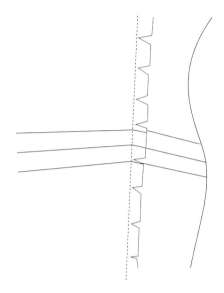

K Pressing the seam allowances toward the facings.

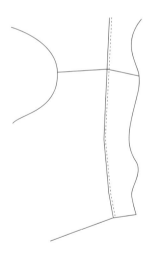

L Edgestitching the facing just inside the seam line.

M Pressing the edge of the neckline from the inside.

SEWING ORDER

It has come to my attention during the writing of this book that some of my construction methods differ from those of standard commercial patterns. This is because I rely heavily on fittings in the sewing process and also like to leave room for future alterations. In this book I'm assuming that you're sewing for yourself or for others on a small scale.

If you have the opportunity to fit a garment you're making for the first time, then I recommend assembling the dress and applying the zipper last, after you know that the center back seam is correct. If you've placed zippers before, you know that putting one into a finished garment is not as easy as putting it into a flat, back section that hasn't been joined at the side seams. So, the first time you sew a garment with your new pattern you'll probably want to put the zipper in after the fitting. In subsequent garments, however, you'll be able to apply the zipper in an earlier, more convenient step.

This same rule also goes for the order of sewing the side seams and the waist seams on a dress. A dress is easier to alter later in the side seams if there is a continuous seam along the underarm to the hem. Some dresses (some would argue all dresses) look better and smoother at the waist seam if there is a continuous seam and therefore an uninterrupted line all the way around the waist. At the end of the day, it's really a matter of what you choose on a case-by-case basis.

One of the benefits of sewing for yourself or for your children is that you have the option of building in room for growth. When you spend a great deal of time on something that's very special to you or for whomever you're making the garment, it's nice to know that it can be used in years to come and possibly by more than one person.

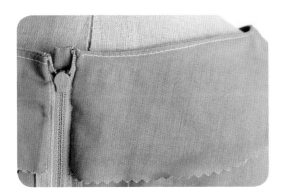

N The ends of the facings blindstitched around the zipper.

STEP 5: Hem the Dress

Our final step is to hem the dress.

1 Pin the pleat insert to the folded edges of the pleat and then sew along each side. Repeat on the other side of the dress.

2 Gently press the pleat area from the outside so that it lies smoothly. Then pin along the top of the pleats to secure them to the dress exterior. Topstitch across this line (see **A**). The dress is now ready to hem.

3 If possible, check the length with a final fitting.

4 Mark the hem evenly all the way around by using a yardstick or another hem-measuring tool. Some tools allow you to place a pin at the same height all around while some let you mark a powdered chalk line; however, a yardstick works just as well. Make sure the marks are even and then take the dress to the ironing board to transfer your markings.

5 Using a straight edge, true up your marking line. If there is a dip in the line, trust the mark from your fitting, as the hemline you copied from the original will vary due to the drape of the fabric as well as the wearer. The bust and derriere make the hemline dip up. Bias seams tend to stretch out over time and make the hemline dip down.

The finished dress.

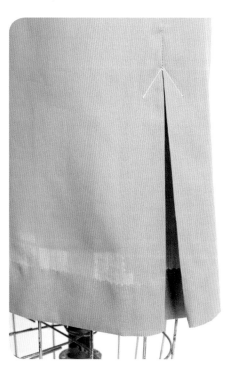

Ⓐ The finished pleat is topstitched both to secure the shape of the pleat and to draw attention to it.

page 86 page 90 page 92 page 94 page 96

Each of these dresses
can be made by
altering the pattern
of the vintage source
dress we re-created
at the beginning of the
chapter.

DRESS VARIATIONS

Here are some variations of the vintage sheath dress we re-created at the
beginning of this chapter. With the basic sloper source dress pattern, you
can alter the neckline, eliminate the darts by shifting them to create a
princess line, play with the height of the waistline, and learn how to make a
fully lined bodice. You can also swap out the skirt of the dress with any of the
skirts from Chapter 2 and create endless variations of the original!

Retro V-Neck Dress

Embrace the retro feel of this V-neck version of our source dress pattern. This dress differs with the source only in the neckline and the sleeves. The fitted waist and narrow skirt of this version of the dress pattern will put a wiggle in your walk.

ALTERING THE BODICE

This dress uses the skirt in its original form and alters the bodice slightly by eliminating the sleeves and then reshaping the armhole for a more flattering sleeveless line.

    The neckline is dropped into a gently curving V-neck and a facing that includes both the neck and armholes is created to provide smooth structure and stability.

1 Begin by creating a V-neck bodice from the original bodice pattern and redraw the neckline as shown in illustration **A**.

2 Cut out the bodice, including fusible interfacing and a new all-in-one facing for the bodice.

3 After making the darts in all your bodice pieces, attach them at the shoulder only, leaving the side seams for later.

THE FACINGS

1 Apply all-in-one facing flat to the neck and armholes before the side seams are sewn. They will maintain a smooth shoulder seam.

2 Attach your facings together at the shoulder seams, leaving the underarm area of the facings unattached. You'll use this method of facing for the entire neck and armholes at the same time when attaching a fully lined bodice in subsequent variation projects.

3 Press open the shoulder seams on both the bodice and the facing.

4 With both your bodice and facing pieces attached at the shoulder seams, lay them out flat, with the right sides together, matching all junctures, such as the shoulder seams and sides. See **B** on page 88.

5 Pin the bodice and facing pieces together using the technique for creating an edge that rolls under (see page 120 in Chapter 4).

6 With both pieces pinned together, sew around the neckline, starting at one center back edge and then stopping at the other.

7 Next sew around each armhole separately, starting from one side seam edge and stopping at the other.

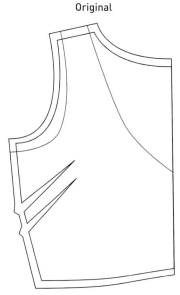

Original

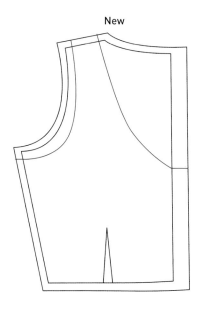

New

A Redrawing the neckline.

By simply altering the source dress pattern into a V-neck and extending the side seams, our source dress quickly transforms into this retro-looking sheath dress.

8 You should now have one flat bodice that's lined but still unattached at the side seams (see **B**).

9 Clip into all the curves and trim the seam allowances. Press open the seams as far as you can. At the shoulder area, where this is impossible, press open on one side first and then press on the other until the seam is pressed open. Edgestitch the facing along the inside of the seam (the side of the seam that will be on the inside of the garment). Be sure to stitch through the facing to the seam allowance, which will ensure that this edge doesn't roll out to the outside of the finished garment.

10 Trim and press the seams where possible. Afterwards, turn the bodice right side out (see **C**).

11 Gently press the neckline and armhole edges from the inside, again, making sure that the seam rolls slightly to the inside.

12 Open the bodice back up and pin each of the side seams together. Pin the bottom edges of the front and back together. Then pin up to the underarm and up through the facing pieces (see **D**).

13 Repeat for the other side of the bodice and then stitch.

14 Press open the underarm seams and turn the bodice back right sides out. You now have clean, finished neck and armhole seams.

THE SKIRT

1 Continue putting the skirt onto the bodice. After you've applied the zipper in the back, turn the dress inside out and fold the edges of the facing piece under so that it just covers the edge of the zipper.

2 Slipstitch the facing to the seam allowance, making sure not to go all the way through to the exterior of the bodice with your stitches.

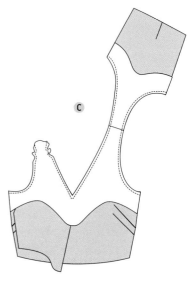

B Facing is applied by stitching all around the neck and arms, leaving the side seams open. **C** Trimming the seams, pressing where possible, edgestitching, and turning the bodice right side out. **D** Sewing the side seams of the bodice and lining in one continuous line.

THE SIDE PLEATS

Ease of movement is maintained with kicky, little side pleats from the original source dress.

1 Extend the side seams as described in Step 3 on page 31.

2 The facing of the pleat is made by measuring the dimension of the full pleat *after* the skirt pieces are sewn together. (Sew with a regular stitch length down to the pleat, backstitching, and then changing to a basting-stitch length and continuing the seam as a basting stitch to baste the pleat together.)

3 Sew the facing to the pleat at both sides, making sure to sew from the top and down or from the bottom and up on both sides after pinning to keep the facing on the straight of grain.

4 Turn to the right side and pin down the pleat. Topstitch either across the top edge of the pleat or at a slight angle.

5 Hem the skirt, turning it up all around—including the pleat in the hem—and then repress the pleat into place after the hem has been sewn.

The side pleat.

A-Line Money Dress

The crinkle texture of this copper sleeveless A-line dress with a ribbon belt is a nice counterpoint to the super-sweet lines of the modified bodice. The silhouette exudes a classic, vintage feel; but the fabric, modified waistline, and scooped neck give it a modern twist. In addition, the bodice is fully lined.

1 Raise the waistline and scoop out the neckline from the source dress pattern (see **A**). Make a duplicate bodice pattern for the lining fabric. Apply it to the outer bodice using the same technique we used when applying the facings in the previous project (see pages 86–88).

2 Sew the darts in both the exterior bodice and lining pieces. Attach at the shoulder seams only the bodice and the lining.

3 While still flat and opened at the side seams, pin the bodice and lining with the right sides together. Then sew around the neckline and each armhole.

4 Clip and press the seams and turn the lined bodice.

5 Edgestitch the neckline and armholes for smooth, clean curves.

6 Sew the side seams onto the outer bodice only. Then slipstitch the lining at the side seams.

7 Hand-finish the lapped zipper to avoid a hard line down the back of the dress. Work the silvery ribbon belt into the center back seam by hand as well and anchor it to the front with a vintage mother-of-pearl buckle (see **B**).

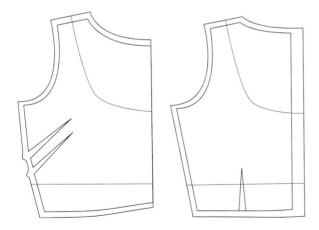

A The waistline is raised and the neckline is scooped out from the original source dress pattern.

B A silvery ribbon belt and mother-of-pearl buckle accent the dress.

The raised waistline and scooped neckline give a classic look to this A-line dress variation.

Inner Audrey Princess Seam Dress

Throw on some kitten heels and a trench and channel your inner Audrey. The texture and body of this black brocade fabric make it a terrific choice for the clean lines of our little black dress. Our original bodice pattern is modified by shifting the bust darts to create a princess seam pattern, which is one of the most versatile and fittable shapes. The princess seam lines are extended down and into the skirt pattern, which gives fullness to the body of the skirt, not just the side seams.

CREATING A PRINCESS SEAM

1 Trace the source bodice pattern onto a new sheet of kraft paper.

2 Make a dot at the bust point. It's usually pretty obvious, but you may need to compare the pattern to a dress form or hold it up to the person you're fitting to determine its exact location. This is the apex of the pattern, the only spot on the bodice that will always need to be flat, because it's the fullest part of the chest. Any darts you make in the bodice pattern must pivot around this point.

3 Take the traced new pieces and draw the princess lines onto the pattern piece. To do this, measure the shoulder seam, find the middle, and make a mark there. Measure the bottom of the bodice piece, find the middle, and make a mark there. Now connect each of these lines to the bust point. This is the rough version of the princess seam line. You'll smooth it out later.

4 Cut out the old dart shapes with paper scissors, extending them, if necessary, all the way to the bust point on each dart.

5 Cut the princess lines you made in Step 2 all the way to the bust point.

6 Shift the old darts closed, as if they had been sewn together, and tape them shut. This will cause the princess lines you just cut to open up (see **A**). You've just shifted the fullness of the bodice from the side seams to above and below the bust. You can use these new darts, above and below the bust, as darts, or divide the piece completely into two pieces and smooth the edges with the design curve ruler to create two new bodice front pieces, which, when sewn together, create a princess line.

7 These are your two new pieces. Name them center front and side front respectively.

8 Note the grain lines on the new pieces.

9 Repeat the same sequence on the back of the bodice pattern pieces, naming them center back and side back.

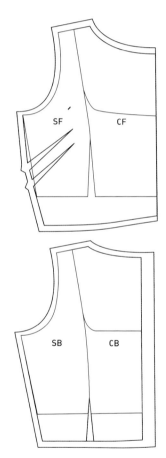

A Shifting the darts create princess seams.

Shifting the darts to make a princess seam converts the source dress into a perfect little black dress, which can be worn for any number of occasions—a long cigarette holder is, of course, optional.

Vintage Shop 'Til You Drop Dress

If you're reading this book you probably love combing through vintage fabrics and findings. This head-turning, vintage-inspired dress was made with a princess pattern bodice and A-line skirt patterns. The red in the bodice and the touch of blue in the belt makes for a charming combination with the bold floral print in the skirt. These elements are pulled together with a vintage buckle and matching buttons in hot-red Bakelite.

CONVERTING THE BODICE

Begin with the princess pattern variation (see the Inner Audrey Princess Seam Dress on page 92). Trace the bodice pattern pieces and then alter the new pattern by squaring the neckline as shown in **A**.

CONVERTING THE SKIRT

1 The skirt is an A-line pattern. Before cutting, make sure that your waistline measurement for the top of the skirt matches the waistline measurement of the bottom of the bodice. This is referred to as "walking" the pattern. You do this to check and make sure the garment is going to be sewn together properly before you cut.

2 Lay the pattern onto the fabric and cut. In this example there is a large print to be matched. Use the same technique for matching this print as used in the Striped A-line Skirt on page 54. In this case it was impossible to match all seams all the way around, so I chose to match the center back seam so that it's more similar to the center front piece, which is cut on the fold and therefore has an uninterrupted pattern. To do this, cut the first side and then take the paper pattern and fold the seam allowance back and lay it next to the cut piece, drawing in the print on the paper pattern where the print should continue. Next, find the same area of print on your fabric and align the paper pattern accordingly so that when the pieces are cut and sewn the print will look as if it's a continuous piece of fabric with no seam (see **B**).

3 Sew the dress, using the lining technique described on page 92.

4 Overlock the hem, turn it up, and machine topstitch.

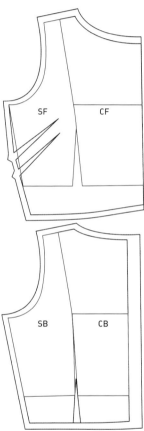

A The new neckline and princess seams of the bodice.

B Matching the print on the center back seam

A bold floral print, princess seams, and square neckline will give you this eye-catching look to show off your vintage findings.

Pin-Up Halter Dress

There is a reason why so many swimsuits have a halter neckline: There aren't many figures I've seen that it doesn't look great on! So, I've taken the princess line version of our bodice and modified it further. You could easily leave it strapless (the princess seam here makes fitting a strapless so much easier), but I've chosen to give it these sassy halter straps. In order to make the straps as stable as possible, I've cut them on the straight of grain of the fabric (remember this is the direction that has the least stretch). The straps were assembled first in the bodice-making process and then sandwiched in between the outer bodice and the bodice lining to create a clean finished interior with no raw edges exposed. The skirt pattern is slashed and spread to create a gathered waistline. Hips . . . what hips? A gathered waistline is very forgiving and very flattering. An A+ in my book!

CONVERTING THE BODICE

1 Begin by making a copy of the princess pattern variation (see the Inner Audrey Princess Seam Dress on page 92). It will serve as the foundation for our halter pattern (see **A**).

2 Align the princess pattern pieces together on a table according to how they will appear when sewn together. Temporarily tape the pattern pieces just above the bust area. Align them so that the center front, side front, side back, and center back are all taped together at the seams just above the bust area. This is where you will make the line delineating the top of the halter.

3 Find the neckline from the square shape on the Vintage Shop 'Til You Drop Dress on page 94. Extend it across the side front pattern piece, making sure you're staying far enough above your **bustline**.

4 Using a curve tool, continue to extend the line, dipping downward to continue under the armhole, around the back pattern pieces, and to the center back.

5 Lay the entire arrangement over a sheet of kraft paper.

6 Draw the halter strap as shown in A. It's a good idea to create the strap pattern at this stage because you can see at which angle the strap will need to be attached and cut it accordingly. Mark the points where the strap will join the bodice and use them as notches when sewing the bodice later.

7 Trace the strap pattern onto the kraft paper using a needle wheel.

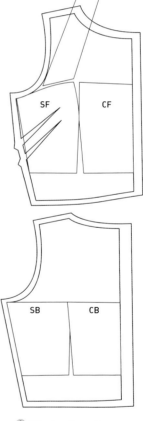

A Altering the princess seam bodice for a strapless or halter.

8 Mark the strap pattern with the straight of grain running parallel to the edge of the strap. This will give the strap more stability. (If you extend the strap up from the bodice pattern piece, it would be on the bias and therefore not as smooth or strong.)

With a modified princess seam halter top and a gathered skirt at the waistline, this dress variation looks perfect on every type of figure.

9 Cut the bodice pattern pieces along the new strapless neckline we've now created. Cut them apart again. Now you have all the new bodice pieces for the halter dress.

10 For a sturdy construction of this bodice, it's a good idea to cut the lining out of the same fabric as the outer bodice (cut two of each of the pieces of the bodice) so that the lining is the same weight as the exterior of the dress. Depending on the thickness of the fabric, you may want to use fusible interfacing on all the outer pieces to give it some body.

CONVERTING THE SKIRT

The skirt consists of two gathered rectangles of fabric sewn at the side seams and gathered along the top edge (see **B**). Determine how wide to make your skirt by measuring the waistline of the dress and doubling it. This will ensure that you have a nice, fully gathered waist (see **C**). If your fabric is unusually thick, consider reducing it to one and a half times the waistline measurement; or if it's super thin, increase it to as much as three times the waist measurement. Doubling is a good place to start, though. The length is simply what you would like the skirt to be measured from the midriff to the desired length along the leg.

ASSEMBLING AND SEWING THE PIECES

1 Sew the strap pieces first, with right sides together. Trim pieces, press them open, and turn. I found that a loop-turning tool is helpful with this step. Just place the long wire into the sewn and pressed strap, catch the hooked end in the seam allowance at the top, and pull the strap right side out. Gently press again from the right side.

2 Stitch the bodice pieces together so that you have a completed bodice and a separate, completed lining.

3 Pin the straps at the notches you made in Step 6 on page 96 (along the top edge outside of the bodice). After pinning, take a look at the way they will adjoin the bodice after they are sewn. Make any corrections in the angle now before you sew. When you're happy with the angle of the straps, sew them onto the bodice.

4 Assemble the skirt by sewing both side seams and then pressing them open. Run two rows of gathering stitches along the top edge, pin the skirt at the waist, and pull the gathering threads to match the waistline of the bodice.

5 Attach the unlined bodice and the skirt at the waist seam.

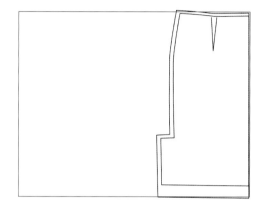

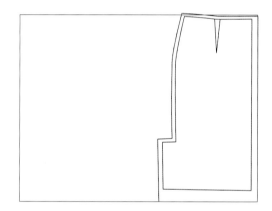

C The skirt pattern expanded to create gathers.

6 Sew the zipper into the center back seam.

7 Pin the bodice lining to the bodice with right sides together and the straps sandwiched between the two layers, pointing down and toward the skirt. Then sew along the top edge.

8 Clip and trim the seam. Press the seam toward the lining and edgestitch along the top edge of the lining $\frac{1}{8}$ inch away from the seam line.

9 Gently press the top edge of the bodice from the inside.

10 Turn the dress inside out and turn the raw edges of the lining. Then slipstitch all around the folded edge, from the top of the inside zipper, down and beside the zipper, across the waist seam, and then back up to the other side of the zipper.

11 Apply a hook and loop to the top of the zipper area to keep the bodice from gaping along the top edge.

12 Check the dress for length and hem.

D The topstitched hem.

B Two gathered rectangles are sewn at the side seams and gathered along the top edge to create the skirt.

CHAPTER 4

PATTERNING
BLOUSES

THE SOURCE BLOUSE

This vintage 1940s silk blouse belonged to my dear friend's mother and fit her beautifully. My friend cherishes it so much that she finds it hard to wear for fear of destroying it. I chose to use the paper rub-off method because of all the details. It's much easier to get an accurate transfer of information if you're able to pin the original garment into a surface, as you can spread the garment out and stabilize it with the pins to make sure it doesn't shift as you're tracing. As you can see, this blouse has ¾-length sleeves with **French cuffs**, a standard pointed collar and facing, which is sometimes referred to as a notched collar, and a hidden button placket. The body is shaped with four pleats in the front and four in the back and the hem is topstitched.

I chose this project because of the collar and cuffs. Once you learn the basic concepts of sewing collars and cuffs you can apply these principles to many projects, such as lapels on a tailored jacket or coat and pocket flaps on jackets, shirt, and pants.

The blouse rub-off is by far the trickiest of all the projects. It has many shaping features that make it difficult to spread flat and pattern everything at once. Take your time with these projects to make sure you're being as precise as possible—and don't be afraid to leave extra seam allowance.

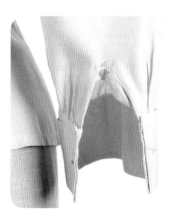

A French cuff sleeve.

A notched collar.

Pleats shape the waist.

The vintage source blouse.

As we did in the last three projects, we'll begin by tracing the garment. As mentioned, I chose the paper rub-off method for this project because of the many shaping details. It's easier to get an exact duplicate when pinning into a work surface, because you're able to smooth the blouse out and pin it down so it doesn't shift as much.

THE FRONT AND BACK

If you'd like to make your facing a part of the blouse front, leave enough paper on the front side for another half of a blouse front. If you look inside this blouse you can tell that the facing extends all the way up and into the shoulder seam—it's actually half the width of the blouse front for this reason (see **A**).

1 Begin by making a straight vertical line on your kraft paper to begin pinning the center front and then a perpendicular line at the bottom of it, making the same L-shape as in the other projects. This will ensure that you're keeping the pattern square. In addition, if the hemline dips down on one side or the other you'll be able to see it right away.

2 Pin the blouse's front edge to the vertical line. Make sure not to pull it out of shape (see **B**).

3 Spread out the blouse front evenly and pin at key points at the underarm, bustline, and the shoulder at the top of the armhole.

4 Continue pinning between the key points. Delineate all the points you'll need to create the pattern, such as anywhere a straight line would curve or change direction.

5 Work around the darts (in our case the pleats) and pin into the dart/pleat line to give you their length and position for later. You'll notice that the blouse does not spread completely flat at the side seams. This is because the pleats are pulling the waistline in. Pinch out the amount that does not lie flat and pin it out of the way. Measure the amount, as it will be used later in determining some of the shaping of the pleats.

6 After you have all the marks along the bottom edge, release any pins you need to continue flattening and pin around the top edge (see **C**). Pin any areas that you'll want to note, such as where the collar joins the neckline, on the paper pattern. Make a sleeve notch by placing a pin at the middle of

A By turning the blouse inside out you see that the facing extends up into the shoulder seam.

the armhole. Note this mark on the blouse front pattern and then later on the sleeve pattern.

7 Remove the blouse front and lightly sketch in your outer edges, connecting the pin holes and making any notes you'll need before you move on (see **D**).

8 Take a look at your blouse and determine if you need to make two separate pattern pieces for the front. If so, continue to trace the other side and make changes as you go. If your blouse doesn't have two different sides, you'll be able to use the same pattern piece for both sides. We're going to eliminate the extra hidden placket from the original blouse and pattern a traditional button-front area that will leave the buttons visible. Both sides are the same except for the pocket and the placket. In our case, the right side overlaps over the left, which is traditional lapping for all women's clothing: Men's clothing laps left over right. I've heard many people say, "Women are always right, and men are left over" as an easy way to remember this.

9 Make a note of the blouse back's center back and draw it on the paper. Draw the bottom perpendicular line to make the L. Align the blouse and first pin around the bottom and then the top edges, as you did for the front (see **E**).

10 Trace the blouse back using the same method as the front, working carefully around the pleats/darts and making marks where you need to transfer information.

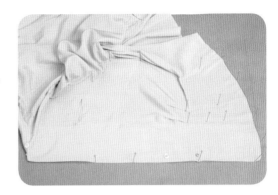

B Pinning the blouse front to the vertical line and its bottom edges.

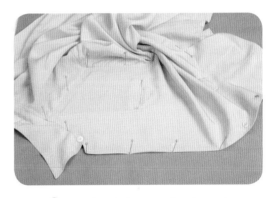

C Releasing the bottom edge pins and pinning along top edge.

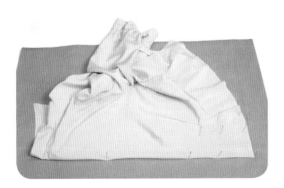

E Pinning the back of the blouse to the L-shape.

D The blouse front pattern traced onto paper.

11 Remove the blouse from the kraft paper and sketch in your marks for the blouse back pattern lightly so that you'll be able to find them later. This is the shape of the blouse with pleats. We'll add in the amount that's sewn out of the pleats into the final pattern later.

THE SLEEVES

Fold a sleeve in half evenly from the underarm.

1 Make a straight line down the middle of another piece of kraft paper and pin the front side of the sleeve to the left of the line. Continue to pattern as we did on the dress sleeve on page 70, making notes of the pins you placed earlier as notches. Note the following:

★ Does the sleeve cap touch the line or is it just a little to the outside of the line? This extra little wedge of fabric eventually will create a slight fullness in the very top of even the most fitted sleeve. It's the ease of the sleeve cap and it is very important to keep in.

★ Feel along the line of the sleeve where it joins the body of the blouse to determine whether the two seams are lining up exactly on top of each other. Is the sleeve symmetrical, allowing you to pattern only one half? Most likely it won't be, and you'll have to first pin through one side and then flip the sleeve over and pin through the other side.

2 Sleeves with cuffs normally have an opening in the sleeve that is finished with a **placket**. Mark (1) where and how long your sleeve and your sleeve placket is and (2) where any gathers at the sleeve cap begin and end. Then remove the pins and flip the sleeve over, matching the folded edge of the sleeve to your pencil line. Pin the sleeve down along the line, making sure to match the top and bottom with the pin marks from the other side.

3 Continue pinning at the relevant points and junctures, including the notch mark you pinned in Step 6 in the front section (see page 104). This will be an important time-saving step in the sewing stage later on.

4 Remove the sleeve and sketch in the lines on the paper pattern.

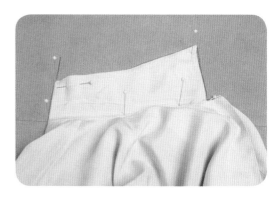
F Pinning the collar to the L-shape.

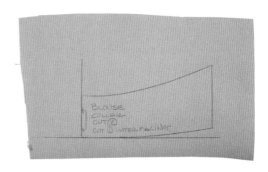
G The paper collar pattern.

THE COLLAR

1 Take a new piece of kraft paper and make an L-shape.

2 Pin the collar in half and then pin the straightest edge to the bottom perpendicular line of the L (see F). Remember to smooth the collar as you pin. This can be used for both the upper and under collar.

3 Trace lightly around the edges to make the shape of the collar.

4 Remove the pins and sketch the collar shape (see G).

THE CUFFS

Begin by marking the vertical center line on a new piece of kraft paper and pinning a cuff to it. You'll need to cut a total of four cuffs from the fabric: One for the inside and outside of each cuff and two for the interfacing (one for each cuff). Don't trace the blouse facing now. You'll use the paper pattern to create the facings so that they will be as similar as possible to the shape of the neckline later in Step 2 on page 120.

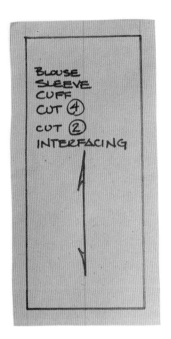

H The paper cuff pattern.

ADDING MEASUREMENTS

Go back and add the pleat or dart measurements to the blouse front and back pattern pieces. Notice how the hemline dips up on the side seam. This is because the pleats/darts pull the side seam in so much that it lifts the hem up. You'll take the amount you pinched out of the waist area in order for the blouse to lie flat on the paper and add that amount back into the hemline. It should bring you back to a square outer edge to the bottom of the pattern piece. Use the same method to add in the amount needed for your pleats/darts.

1 Measure the pleats/darts from the inside of the blouse, just as you did for darts in Chapter 2 (see page 34). Then measure this same amount from the edge of the traced-in side seam.

2 Draw in the new side seam. It should be fairly straight.

3 Add the pleats/darts to the pattern by duplicating your measurements from the inside of the blouse front from Step 1. In many cases you'll need to disregard the traced lines completely and draw in fresh darts or pleats that maintain the distance from each outer edge of the pattern piece and from each other. Don't obsess if you are a little off the tracing marks. Garments get tweaked and stretched from wear. At a certain point you need to check your measurements, make sure the new pattern is balanced, square, and symmetrical, and then move on.

4 Look carefully at the placket area of the sleeve cuff. Using your tape measure or ruler, measure the length and width of the placket and then draw a rectangle on your paper pattern for those measurements (see I).

5 Draw in all the surfaces of the placket: (1) the front side, (2) the back side, and (3) a ¼-inch seam allowance on each edge. At this stage add the seam allowance to where the placket will extend with the sleeve into the seam allowance that's covered by the cuff (½–⅝ inch, or the same as your seam allowance for the sleeves).

6 Mark the pattern piece "Sleeve Placket" and cut two, one for each sleeve (see J).

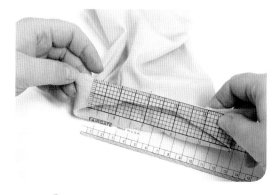

I Measuring the placket with a gridded ruler.

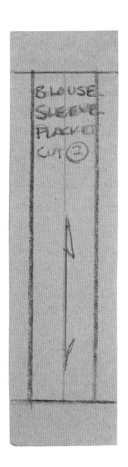

J The finished placket pattern with added seem allowances.

Once you master rubbing off blouses, this variation can easily be made (see page 134).

STEP 2: Create the Blouse Pattern

Now you have all your traced blouse pattern pieces. If the original blouse fits well and you don't need to change anything, you can move on to "Adding Seam Allowances" (see page 112). If you would like to enlarge or shrink the pattern, this is the stage to slash and spread the paper pattern.

ALTERING THE BLOUSE PATTERN

For our blouse we need to slash and spread along the basic princess lines and bust lines, as shown in photo **A**. If you need to add 3 inches to your basic bust measurements, you would divide those additional 3 inches by 4 (two front halves and two back halves), adding ¾ inch to each of the four pieces. You can split both the front and back pieces along the center and spread, or you could divide the ¾ inch in half again and add ³/₈ inch to the outside edges of both the front and back pieces. This is similar to commercial patterns that have multiple sizes included in one pattern. The sizes are merely fractions of an inch apart when you look at them seam by seam.

I don't recommend using this method if you're adding more that a ½ inch to each seam, as the garment features will become distorted if you try to spread too much in the neckline, for example. It will grow even larger when you add to the center front and center back. In such a case you would need to slash and spread the piece through the shoulder's intersection. Fortunately, because we are usually rubbing off a garment that either fits us or is only slightly off, this should not be a problem. If you need to do more extensive alterations to the pattern, there are many great books on the subject that you can find in the Resources section on page 164.

1 I add ¾ inch to the front piece. You can see how cutting two of this expanded pattern piece would add up to a total of 1½ inches in the total front. Doing the same to the back would give us the other 1½ inches to make 3 inches total.

2 After you've adjusted the body, you'll need to transfer any changes to the collar piece. The changes we've made to this blouse pattern don't affect the neckline or collar pieces because of where the piece is spread. If you ever need to add to the center back line of a garment, it will affect the neckline measurement and you'll need to adjust the collar pattern to match the new neck opening. Measure the new neckline by matching the front and back pattern pieces at the shoulder seam and measuring around the neckline with a tape measure. Make a note of the measurement on the paper so you can have it for future reference. Spread the collar piece on the center back

A The blouse front pattern, slashed and spread, adding in spread.

ADVANCED SLASHING AND SPREADING

More advanced readers may notice that ideally we would add only to the area that needs to be expanded and would therefore have extensive measurements documenting the exact width of the wearer's bust front and bust back, allowing us to perfectly customize the final pattern. We would also leave the shoulder seam at the same measurement and spread only through the bust, narrowing the spread back again at the hemline. In this example, however, we want to show the simplest version of the slash-and-spread technique.

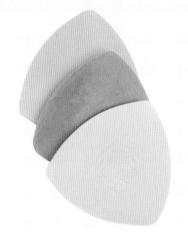

line. Extend it so that it matches the new dimension of the neckline you've just measured. Again, the adjustment we've made to the body of the blouse won't actually affect the sleeve measurement because the armhole wasn't included in the spreading of the pieces. However, if you ever need to slash and spread a sleeve if the original is too tight you would spread the pattern down the center as in photo **A**.

3 Measure the new armhole by matching the front and back pattern pieces at the shoulder seam. Transfer any addition to the sleeve and then to the cuff. Remember that there is always a little ease in the sleeve cap in a set-in sleeve. Make sure you maintain the amount of ease when transferring the new armhole and sleeve cap measurements. If these two measurements are exactly the same, the sleeve might be very easy to sew in, but the look of the sleeve will be tight across the top edge. This is a very common mistake among rookie patternmakers. Here's another example of where you could cut the sleeve pattern down the center, but if the armhole is okay you could just spread the sleeve pattern over the upper arm area, tapering it back to the original lines at the armhole and the sleeve hem. So, instead of a straight strip all the way down the pattern piece, the spread section would form an elongated diamond shape. This would make the sleeve larger only where you need it instead of a whole size up (see **B**).

B Adding fullness and ease to the sleeve pattern.

4 At this stage you can make any style variations you would like. See pages 125–137 for some variations of our source blouse. You can do any of the following:

★ Shorten or lengthen the sleeves

★ Add more or fewer gathers to the sleeves

★ Remove the sleeves or the collar and add facings

★ Add a peplum (a little kicky skirt piece) to the bodice

★ Add seams or remove pleats/darts

★ Reshape the collar

CREATING THE FACINGS

You'll now need to make facing patterns for the front of the blouse.

1 Take the front pattern piece and measure 2 to 3 inches from the center front edge and all the way up the front of the pattern. Then measure the same amount all around the curve of the neckline (see C).

2 Take a curve tool and smooth out the juncture of the curved and straight lines if you like.

3 Next, fold your pattern piece along the front edge so that there is kraft paper doubled behind the area you just drew. If you'd like the facing to be a separate pattern, you can just place a separate piece of kraft paper under it and make a facing pattern that's independent of the blouse front. Trace through the pattern along the facing line you just measured using a needle wheel (see D).

4 Unfold the kraft paper and connect the dots from the needle wheel line on the traced facing extension. Make a notch at the fold line so that you'll know where to fold the facing back during the sewing stage (see E).

ADDING SEAM ALLOWANCES

Now that you've made all the alterations to the paper pattern, add the seam allowances as was done in the previous projects (see F). When finished, you're now ready to cut the fabric. Check the pattern pieces for grain lines, notches, and the specific pattern's name.

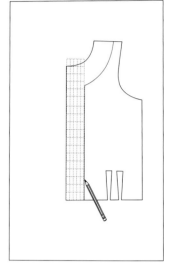

C Measuring for facing.

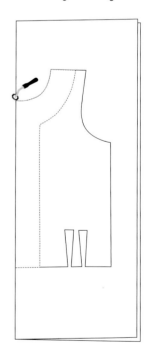

D Tracing the facing area with a needle wheel.

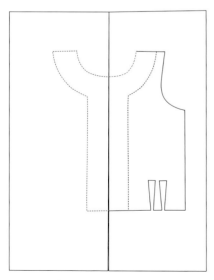

E The blouse front with facing added.

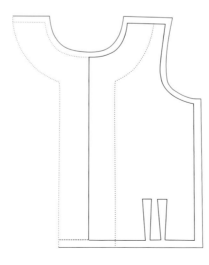

F Adding seam allowances.

STEP 4: Cut the Fabric

Prewash the fabric, press if needed, and lay it out on your cutting surface.

1 Taking into account fold lines and any pattern you must match, lay out the pattern pieces. Measure the grain lines to the edge of the fabric to make sure the pieces are straight and square to the grain line of the fabric. Weight the paper pattern pieces.

2 Using your rotary cutter, cut out all pieces, noticing which side you're working on and the number of pieces to cut for the collar and cuffs.

3 Place the pieces aside as you cut and then cut the interfacing pieces for the collar, cuffs, and facings.

4 Using tracing paper and a tracing wheel, transfer the markings for pleats/darts, notches, buttonholes, and buttons. To mark them on the wrong side of the fabric, fold the paper in half with the chalky or waxy side visible. Then slide the folded paper between the pieces of fabric. As seen on page 41, use the tracing wheel to mark a dart or other notation, pressing firmly to make sure you're marking the bottom layer of fabric effectively. Repeat for all the other markings that need to be on the wrong side of the fabric.

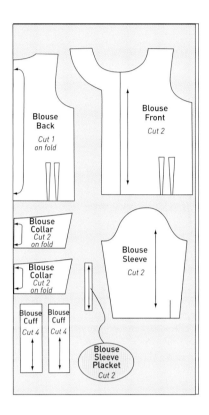

ALTERNATE METHOD FOR MARKING DARTS/PLEATS AND NOTCHES

If you're making a pattern for multiple uses, you may want to cut out the dart/pleat shape so that you can simply trace around it using either chalk, disappearing marker, or a marking pencil. To do this, cover the entire dart/pleat area with tape (this is one of the reasons I like to use ¾-inch tape in my dispenser). Then cut out the dart/pleat shape with paper scissors or an X-Acto knife. This gives a reinforced edge to trace against and helps the pattern last longer.

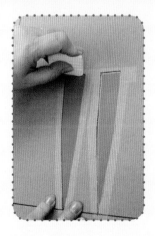

Marking through the taped and cut-out dart/pleat stencil with chalk.

STEP 5: Sew the Blouse

Lay out all your pieces and assess the project. To begin, apply fusible interfacing to the collar, facing, and cuff pieces and set them aside. Use the lightest-weight interfacing you can find to create a soft finished product.

COLLAR TRICK

Here's a little trick to use whenever you're sewing two pieces together that are exactly the same.

1 Pin the two pieces, right sides together (see **A**). Scoot the edges of the under collar piece, which are facing away from the outside of the garment when finished, to the outside of the other piece, creating ⅛ inch of difference all around the edge. The difference is so little that the two pieces can easily be joined without any puckering or gathers, yet it's just enough for the seam to roll gently toward the slightly smaller under collar piece (see **B**). This is often taught in tailoring. When making a tailored jacket, you'd actually trim the under collar piece by ⅛ inch; however, many of the ladies I've worked with over the years taught me to cheat the edges out while pinning. Instead of cutting the ⅛ inch from the edge, simply shift the pieces so that the one you'd like to be smaller is hanging out and around the outside edge of the one you want to be larger. Then, when you sew, you're in effect sewing one ⅛ inch smaller and getting the same result as trimming the edges. These little tricks make a difference in the lay of the final garment to create a refined finish.

2 Stitch the collar with the seam allowance that you added in the pattern. Trim the edges and corners as shown in the clipping corners section on page 25. Press and turn (see **C**).

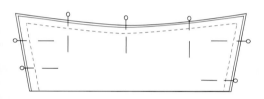

Ⓐ Pinning the collar pieces.

Ⓑ The seam of the finished collar should roll slightly to the underside.

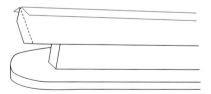

Ⓒ Pressing the collar open on a tailor's board.

CUFFS, PART 1

Take the cuff pieces with the interfacing applied and measure the length of your seam allowance.

1 Press the bottom edge up without the interfacing so that when you sew the two cuff pieces together this edge will be caught in the seams (going in the right direction). This will cut some bulk later in the process (see **A**).

2 Stitch around the edges of the cuff.

3 Trim (see **B**), press, and turn. Set the cuffs aside for later (see **C**).

PLEATS AND DARTS

Take all the pieces with pleats or darts and pin them. Take them to the sewing machine and stitch all, one after the other. Then take all of the pleats or darts and press them. Set aside.

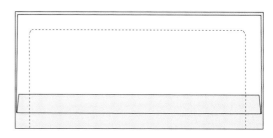

A Folding the seam allowance up and on the un-interfaced side of the cuff up before sewing the cuff together will make finishing the cuff and sleeve easier.

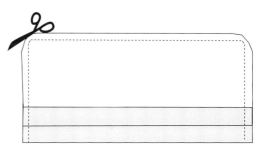

B Trimming the seam allowances from the cuff before pressing.

C The finished cuff ready to be applied to the sleeve.

SHOULDER SEAMS

Next, we will stitch the shoulder seams. Pin the blouse fronts to the blouse backs at the shoulder seams and stitch. Next, press open and finish the edges. Now that you have a neck opening, make a straight machine stitch all the way around the neckline and just to the inside of the seam allowance (see D).

SIDE SEAMS

Pin the side seam with the right sides together. Stitch the side seams and press open. Finish the seams by either pinking or using an overlock machine (see E).

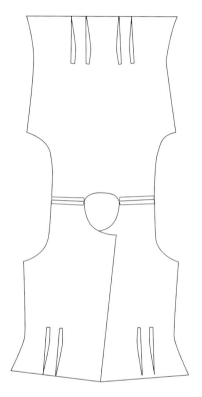

D Stitching, pressing, and finishing the shoulder seams.

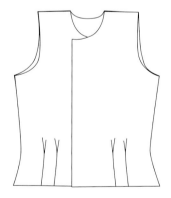

E Sewing the side seams.

SLEEVES

1 Set the machine stitch to basting length (3.4–5) and stitch the easestitching line at the sleeve caps and the cuff edge (see **F**).

2 Cut the openings at the bottom of the sleeves where the placket goes (see **G**).

3 Take the placket pieces and pin them to the edge of the slit (see **H**).

4 Take the packet pieces to your sewing machine and stitch along the edge at 1/4–1/8 inch, making sure to clip any additional amount into the point so that the opening moves freely (see **I**).

5 Fold in the edge of the placket and press. Then fold it again and pin. Hand baste or pin the edge down so that it completely covers the stitching line. Turn it to the right side and machine topstitch the edge down. Repeat with the other sleeve and then press both (see **J**).

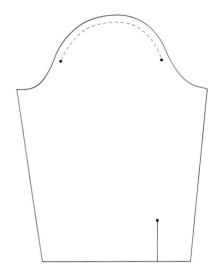

F Stitching around the sleeve cap for ease.

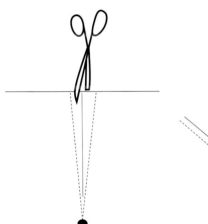

G Cutting an opening into the sleeve for the placket.

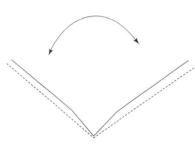

H Spreading the openings for the placket so they can be attached in a straight line.

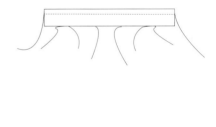

I Stitching the placket to the open edge.

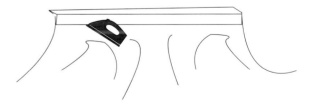

J Folding, pressing, and stitching in the ditch from the outside, making sure to catch a scant amount of the folded edge in the stitching on the back side.

CUFFS, PART 2

Take the cuffs we set aside earlier. We will now attach them to the sleeves.

1 Sew the underarm seams of each sleeve (see **K**). Press them open and finish.

2 Pin the cuff to the sleeve at the edges of the seam allowances. At this point we need to check the source blouse and determine in which direction all of the placket pieces and pleats need to go. It can be very frustrating to sew a cuff onto a sleeve and then the sleeve into the garment, only to find that the placket was sewn in backwards.

3 Fold the pleats into the sleeve as determined by the notches. Take a look at the source blouse and check the proper direction and spacing. Pin the center of the cuff and then pin between the two pins. Anchor the bobbin thread by pulling the threads from the other side to create the gathers, shifting them accordingly to make sure they are distributed evenly. Pin this edge into place. Take it to your sewing machine and change the stitch length back to regular stitching (2.5–3) and sew the cuff to the sleeve (see **L**).

4 Repeat for the other sleeve.

5 Press the seam allowances toward the cuffs.

6 Baste the inner cuff where the cuff and sleeve meet. Topstitch from the outside or slipstitch by hand from the inside to finish and press (see **M**).

7 Take the sleeves you set aside and set in the sleeves as shown in Chapter 3 (see page 80).

8 Turn your blouse body inside out, but keep the sleeves right side out. Pin the sleeve into the armhole as we did in Chapter 3 (see page 80). Pin first at the underarm and shoulder. Then pin at the notches at 9 o'clock and 3 o'clock. Then pin between all those points, continuing in this manner until the sleeve is distributed all the way around the armhole. Anchor the gathering thread on one end and then gently pull the bobbin thread until the dimension of the sleeve cap fits nicely into the armhole. Pin the gathers in place.

9 Begin at the underarm point and stitch the sleeve onto the bodice at a 2.5–3 stitch length.

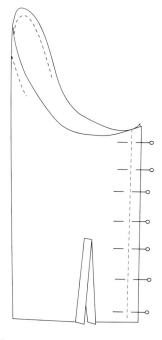

K Sewing the sleeve seams.

10 Repeat with the other sleeve.

11 Try on the blouse for fit before you finish.

12 If the sleeves look good to you, press the seam allowances toward the sleeve. Pink or overlock the seams.

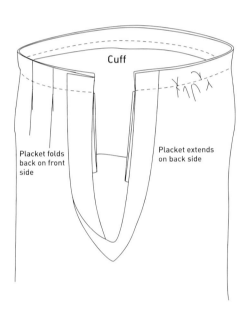

Cuff

Placket folds back on front side

Placket extends on back side

Ⓛ The cuff stitched onto the sleeve.

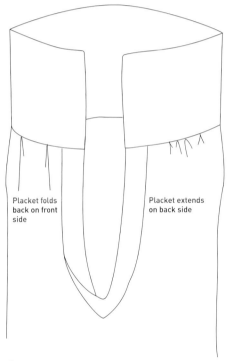

Placket folds back on front side

Placket extends on back side

Ⓜ Topstitch from the outside or slipstitch by hand from the inside to finish.

FACINGS AND UPPER COLLAR

Take the assembled collar and pin it to the neckline, matching the center notches on each piece.

1 Fold both facings along front edge notches with right sides together. Covering the edges of the collar piece, pin.

2 Fold the edges of the facing piece at the shoulder seams so that they will be turned under when the neckline is stitched.

3 Take a look at the neckline area that's now not covered by facing. This area is going to be treated differently because we only need to sew the under collar side to the blouse neckline and the upper collar edge needs to be left free to cover the seam to finish. Clip into the upper collar seam allowances at the shoulder seams of the collar so that it can be tucked out of the way. Pin this flap, which is open now away from the stitching line, and repin the area to be stitched. This little trick will allow you to sew all the way from front edge to front edge and all around the neckline in one continuous pass without stopping to sew the unfaced edge separately.

4 Machine-stitch the facing and collar all the way around.

5 Trim the seams. Press the seams open using a tailor's board. Turn and press from the outside.

6 Fold up and pin the remaining loose collar seam to the neckline edge and the facing ends to the shoulder seams and stitch with a blindstitch. Gently press these hand-stitched areas (see N).

7 Try on the blouse and check the buttonhole placement (see O).

8 Using the manufacturer's instructions for your sewing machine, add your buttonholes to the blouse front and cuffs (see P).

N The blouse inside out on a form, showing the facing and under collar edges hand-finished.

O Making sure there is a buttonhole at the bustline.

BUTTONHOLE PLACEMENT

The fullest part of the bust is a stress point, so you want to make sure that a button falls along this line. Without one, the blouse front may gap across the bust when worn. You'll need to adjust the button placement to accommodate this. Move the buttonhole nearest to the bustline and redistribute the other buttonholes evenly. A good rule of thumb is about 3 inches apart, but it depends on the scale of the buttons and the garment. Another design rule of thumb is to favor an odd number of buttons over an even number if you need to choose. It's one of those golden rules of proportion—just like a rectangle being more pleasing to the eye than a square. Of course, as in all things, you're the designer, so in the end it's up to you.

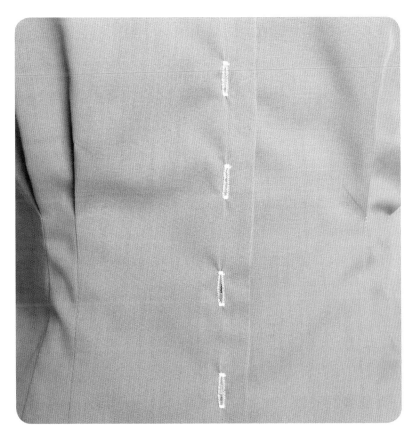

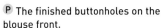 The finished buttonholes on the blouse front.

Our final step is to hem the blouse and apply the buttons.

1 With an invisible marker, make a line ¼ inch from the edge of the hem and press up. Press the line up again (see **A**).

2 Either pin or baste the hem up to prepare for the topstitching. (This is when it pays to do a little basting—especially if you're a perfectionist.) Finish with a topstitch (see **B**).

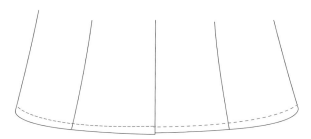

B Topstitching the hem all around.

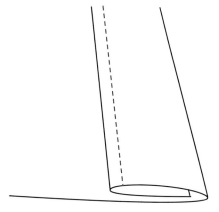

A Turning the hem up ¼ inch and then another ¼ inch.

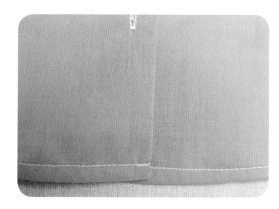

The finished hem.

TOPSTITCHING

Another favorite tip for beautiful finishing is to use rayon thread for topstitching. The thread has a nice luster and gives a very refined look.

3 Match the blouse fronts as when closed. Lightly mark the button placement through the buttonholes (see **C**).

4 Apply the buttons to the front of the blouse as marked in Step 1.

5 Make cuff links for the sleeves by sewing two buttons together (see **D**) and then wrapping those threads with a blanket stitch between the two buttons (see **E**).

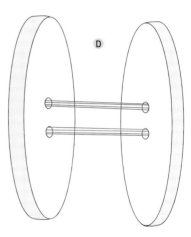

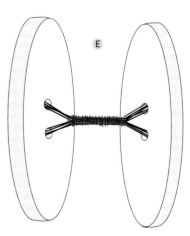

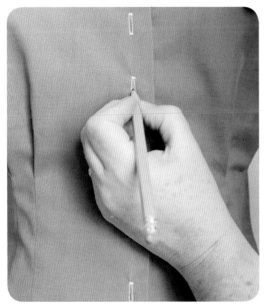

C Overlapping the blouse fronts as they will be worn, marking the buttonholes, and marking the placement of the buttons through the holes.

The finished sleeve cuff with button cuff links.

D Sewing two buttons together to make cuff links. **E** Wrap the shank between the buttons with a blanket stitch.

The finished blouse.

page 126   page 128   page 130   page 132   page 134

From a flowing tunic to a 1950s-inspired halter top, each variation of the source blouse above can easily be made.

BLOUSE VARIATIONS

The simplicity and classic cut of our source blouse is a great template to begin playing with shape and detail in the following design variations. By manipulating pleats into darts, creating princess lines, and shortening—or even removing sleeves—you can achieve dramatically different results and learn some clever finishing tricks along the way.

Green Apple Blouse with Cuffs

Our original blouse pattern is thoroughly modernized with this apple-green cotton print. The crisp lines of the collar, soft pleats, and simplified three-quarter inch sleeve make this a go-to top for everyday. The original blouse had no interfacing in the collar and facings. I've continued that here, because this sturdy, versatile cotton is dense enough to stand up to a buttonhole all by itself and still be soft and cozy.

MAKING A REGULAR CUFF

The only alteration to the pattern is that I made the cuff into a regular cuff instead of the original French cuff.

Divide the source blouse cuff pattern in half lengthwise to eliminate the folded-up portion of the French cuff. Instead of making the four buttonholes required to put the cuff link through both sides of the cuff, you only need to make a buttonhole on the front of the cuff and then place a button on the back of the cuff. Cuffs normally lap from the front to the back.

MAKING A SHANK

If you prefer a regular button, creating a shank will allow for a nicer button placket.

1 Double a piece of thread and put both ends through a needle and knot.

2 Place the button on the mark where you'd like to apply it. Place a standard toothpick across the button.

3 Sew on the button, catching the toothpick in the loops over the button.

4 After a couple of passes, work the needle through the button and between the button and blouse.

5 Remove the toothpick. Loop the thread twice around the excess "shank" of threads that result from having removed the toothpick and then into the fabric. Knot on the inside of the blouse.

A three-quarter sleeve with regular cuff.

Our source blouse pattern is modified into a three-quarter length sleeve with a regular cuff in a pretty green print.

Little Black Blouse with Darts

This version of our source blouse is made in an amazing bamboo fabric that has the texture of linen and the finish of satin organza. The French cuffs from our original source pattern remain, but the pleats are modified into simple darts. You can use the same buttons as the front of the blouse for cuff links, create your own, or find a vintage pair. This blouse transitions from day to evening seamlessly!

CONVERTING THE SOURCE BLOUSE PATTERN

1 Trace the source sleeve pattern onto a separate sheet of kraft paper.

2 Extend the pleat lines and convert them into darts so that they taper just below the bust (see **A**). If you would like a less–fitted-looking silhouette, eliminate one dart in each pattern.

MAKING CUFF LINKS

1 Sew two buttons together with a double-threaded needle leaving a ¼-inch gap between the buttons (see **B**).

2 Wrap the threads connecting the two buttons to make a shank (see **C**).

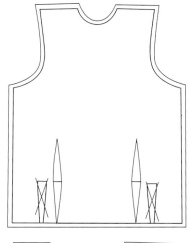

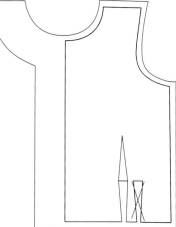

A The new pattern with darts.

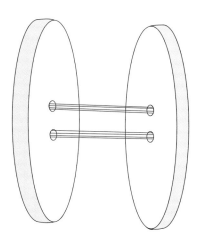

B Two buttons sewn with a double thread.

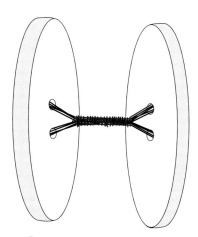

C Wrapping the thread to make a shank.

The pleats that shaped our source blouse pattern are made into darts to make this chic black blouse variation.

Cap Sleeve Summer Sky Blouse

This breezy top takes the pattern we used in the previous blouse variation (see page 128), which uses darts instead of pleats to shape the bodice. The cap sleeve is made by only using part of the sleeve pattern of the source blouse. The sleeve is attached and the armhole bound with a bias strip of the same fabric. Lastly, the points are rounded on the collar pattern for a softer-looking appeal.

MAKING THE CAP SLEEVE AND ROUNDED COLLAR

1 Trace only the sleeve cap (see **A**).

2 Round the points of the collar pattern and sew (see **B**).

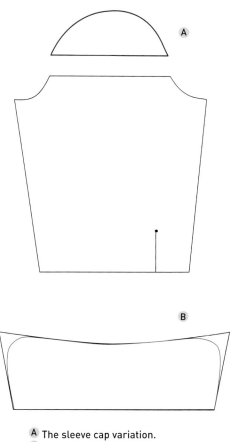

The cap sleeve and rounded collar.

A The sleeve cap variation.
B Rounding the collar points.

This baby blue cap sleeve variation also uses darts instead of pleats for shaping. Only the cap of the sleeve pattern is altered for a sweet little sleeve.

Rock-a-billy Halter Top

Ratchet up the retro by converting our source blouse into a rockin'
1950s-inspired halter top. Make it up in a candy-colored fabric and add
some decorative buttons for a vintage feel.

CONVERTING THE SOURCE BLOUSE PATTERN

1 Trace the original blouse pattern front and back onto another
sheet of kraft paper.

2 Using a curved ruler, extend the darts up into the armhole for a
more fitted line so the upper edge of the blouse won't gape open
(see **A**). Adding these extra seams allows you to fit the halter top
more easily.

3 Draw a line from the underarm up to the neck, shaping it with
the design curve. Make the same alterations to the back pattern
piece (see **B**).

4 Cut and sew, making accommodations for the change in the
collar and facing area as you clip and turn.

5 Reinforce the new edge with a line of twill tape and bind with
ready-made, double-fold bias tape. The bias taped edge is hidden
under the collar in the back (see **C**).

6 Apply bias tape to the raw edge and twill tape just along the
stitching line. The twill keeps the edge from stretching (see **D**).
Then fold the bias tape to the backside and topstitch all around
(see **E**).

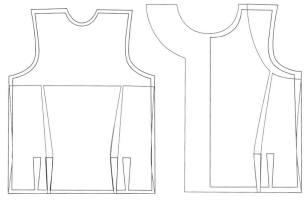

A Extending the pleat lines into the armhole.

B Using a curve tool to make a halter line.

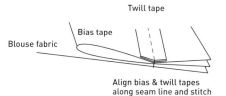

Twill tape

Bias tape

Blouse fabric

Align bias & twill tapes along seam line and stitch

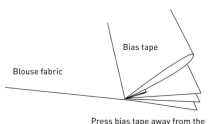

Bias tape

Blouse fabric

Press bias tape away from the outside to enclose the top edge of the blouse

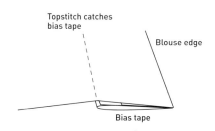

Topstitch catches bias tape

Blouse edge

Bias tape

E The bias tape topstitched
all around the new edge of the
halter.

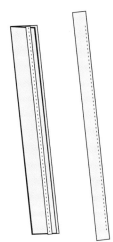

D The binding and facing edge
of the halter.

C Reinforcing the new edge
with twill tape and binding with
bias tape.

This coral halter variation uses an altered version of the source pattern for a rockin' midcentury feel.

Shanti Tunic

Here, the basic blouse pattern is simplified by using only its outer shape, opening the neckline, creating a facing, and eliminating all of the shaping details. The sleeve cuff is eliminated, and the sleeve is finished with hemstitching. A simple shape like this is a great place to try heirloom-sewing stitches, like a hemstitch, for example. A simple **zigzag** stitch, made with a wing needle, creates tiny holes that are reminiscent of vintage linens. Further ease is added with slits up the sides, and the top and hem is finished with mitered corners.

CONVERTING THE SOURCE BLOUSE PATTERN

1 Lengthen the basic blouse pattern to make a simple tunic shape (see **A**).

2 Drop the neckline a couple of inches for a more curved neck opening. Then create a neck facing as seen on page 72 (see **B**).

3 Apply the facing to the tunic edge (see **C**).

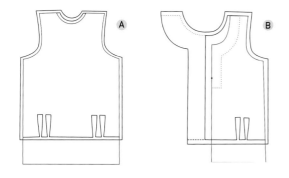

A Converting the basic block of the source blouse. **B** Dropping the neckline. **C** Applying the neck facings.

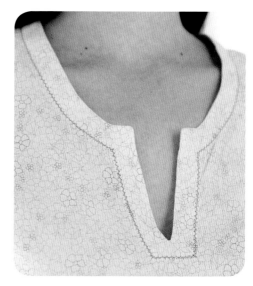

The new neckline.

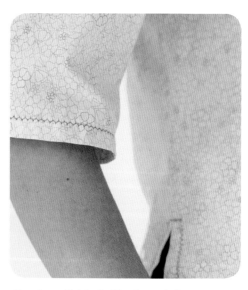

The sleeve finished with a hemstitch.

Elongating the source blouse pattern into a simple tunic shape and using an heirloom hemstitch creates this timeless—and relaxed—blouse variation.

MITERING THE HEM

1 This style of blouse often has slits along the side seams for ease of movement. We will need to miter the corners of the slits.

2 Prepare the hem to be mitered by folding the raw edges together and making a small clip into the point where the edges intersect (see **D**).

3 Open up the folded edges. There should be two fold lines that intersect. The intersection represents the corner. There will also be the two clip marks that represent the intersection of the two fold lines (see **E**).

4 Make a chalk line between the two clips, making sure that the line intersects the corner point (see **F**).

5 Fold the piece with right sides together on the diagonal so that the two clip marks meet (see **G**). Match the lines by pinning into one side and checking that it comes out on the line on the other side. Pin and stitch this line.

6 Trim away the excess from the seam, leaving about a ¼ inch, but less toward the corner point (see **H**).

7 Flip the seam right side out and press gently (see **I**).

8 Apply the hemstitching by first making a long machine-basting stitch along the folded edge of the hem all the way around (see **J**). This is to temporarily hold the hem in place while you finish with the hemstitch. Substitute the wing needle for the standard machine needle in your machine (see **K**). Make a few samples of varying stitch lengths and widths on a piece of the scrap fabric. When you're confident that your machine is set at a pleasing length and width, make the hemstitch all around. I used a decorative rayon embroidery thread and a simple zigzag stitch. You can experiment with various threads to achieve many different effects.

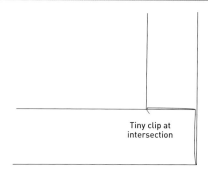

D Preparing the hem.

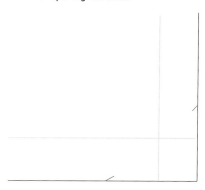

E The intersection representing the corner.

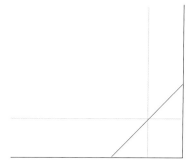

F The chalk line between the two clips.

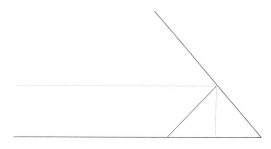

G The right sides together and on the diagonal.

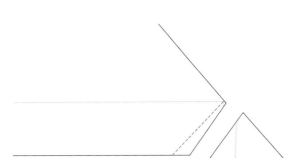

H Trimming away the excess.

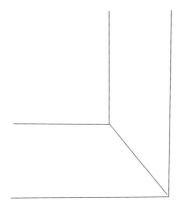

I The seam right side out.

J Hemstitching all around the edges.

K A wing needle.

137

CHAPTER 5

PATTERNING HANDBAGS

THE SOURCE HANDBAG

This vintage 1960s Kelly handbag in navy blue vinyl is a very simple shape that can be duplicated in a variety of sizes and fabric treatments. It has a classic ladylike feel that's both timeless and definitively midcentury fabulous. I can picture it blown up to three times its size and secured with a clasp, zipper, or magnetic closure. It also lends itself to a variety of handles from fabric and leather to molded acrylic and bamboo.

Our source handbag closes with what is often referred to as a "kiss clasp." The front of the handbag is divided into five pieces that can be made in contrasting fabrics if you like. The interior is lined, but there is no pocket—add one or several as needed.

Our vintage source handbag.

The front has five pieced sections.

The handbag has a simple lining with no
pockets or dividers.

A "kiss clasp" closure.

STEP 1: Trace the Handbag

Because the handbag is a three-dimensional object—and we don't want to take it apart to make a new one—the best patterning method to use is the the fabric rub-off. Use a tracing fabric that's flexible but has a little body for easier draping. As mentioned earlier, muslin is the most commonly used fabric for this purpose, but I decided to use Do-Sew, both because its transparency works well for the purpose of demonstration and because it's sturdy enough to withstand some handling while allowing you to see the outline of what you're tracing very easily.

1 Gather tracing fabric, pins, scissors, pencil, and painter's tape. It's good to use a tape that won't damage the original handbag, especially if you're working with a delicate, older vintage piece like our source bag.

2 Cut a piece of tracing fabric that will easily cover the entire handbag.

3 Place the handbag onto the tracing fabric and pull up the ends. Pin the fabric loosely around the sides and top as pictured in photo **A** so that the fabric is flat against the bag without any wrinkles. Then pin for a more snug fit until you have "upholstered" the handbag with tracing fabric.

4 Take a pencil and trace all the seams, making sure to mark the seam on each piece of fabric (see **B**).

5 Note in pencil all the junctures you'll sew later.

6 This handbag has a multipieced front, but we just want to get the overall shape and note where the seams are. Later, we'll create the patterns for the individual pieces by tracing each section onto a separate sheet of kraft paper and then adding seam allowances to the individual pattern pieces. This way we have a master handbag front piece—in case you'd like to make it without the piecing in another version. The basic handbag pattern will also serve as the template for the lining. If you can easily flip your handbag inside out, you can create the lining pattern the same way you did for the outside; but if the lining is the same shape as the exterior, you can use the exterior pattern for your lining as well. You'll want to decrease the lining pattern by ⅛ to ¼ inch as discuss in the "Collar Trick" on page 114.

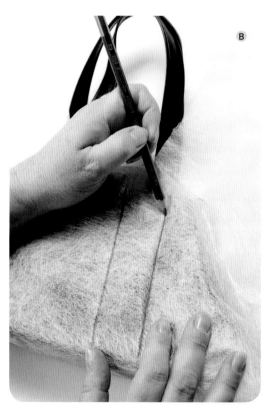

A Cutting a piece of Do-Sew that's big enough to wrap around the bag. Pull up the edges and pin.
B Marking all the seams.

7 Pattern one of the side pieces the same way, using the tape to hold the fabric taut against the bag while you're tracing the seam lines.

STEP 2: Create the Pattern

After tracing the handbag, we're ready to move on to creating the pattern.

1 Separate all the pattern pieces and using a needle wheel and pattern weights, trace the shapes onto a piece of kraft paper (see **A**).

2 Label all the pattern pieces and transfer any notches, grain lines, and cutting instructions to the kraft paper piece (see **B**).

3 If the handles are symmetrical, rectangular shapes, as in our source handbag, you can simply measure them and draw your handle pattern onto the kraft paper using your measurements, ruler, and pencil.

4 Before you add seam allowances, make any style or size changes you'd like.

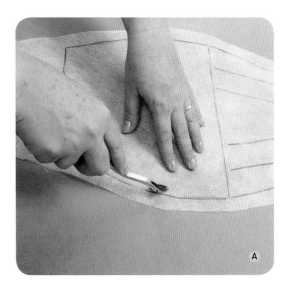

A

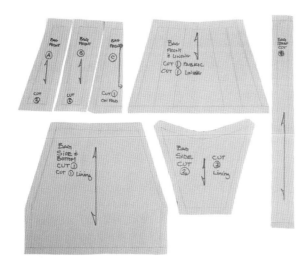

B

A Transferring the shape and information from the tracing fabric to kraft paper with a needle wheel.
B The finished paper pattern for the handbag with seam allowances, grain lines, and individual pieces labeled.

LEARNING THROUGH INVESTIGATION

Look at how the handles of your handbag are finished. Are they a simple tube that has one seam and then turned, pressed, and topstitched? Since the vinyl of our source handbag is so stiff, the vinyl was most likely glued and then stitched. You may choose how to finish your handles according to the thickness and maneuverability of your fabric. The possibilities are endless.

Take into account any pattern or nap your fabric may have. Place any dominant motif in a way that will be desirable in the finished bag. If needed, place weights as you cut.

1 Lay out the pattern pieces (see **A**).

2 Mark around all the pieces with tailor's chalk or pencil.

3 Cut out all of the handbag and lining pattern pieces. If your bag needs inner structure, cut out heavy-duty interfacing and flat lining pieces from the same patterns for any pieces you would like to reinforce (see "A Note about Flat Lining and Interfacing" on page 145).

A Lay out the pieces carefully and note the grain line and direction of any nap.

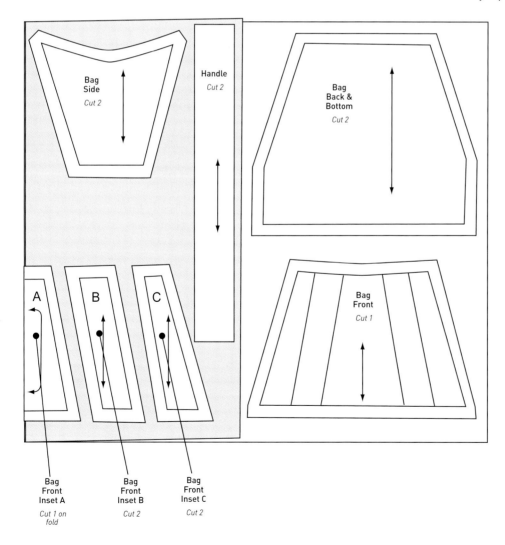

I use a technique called flat lining that's common in theatrical costume construction but may not be familiar to the general sewing public. You flat line a project by sewing a less expensive and usually sturdier fabric to the fashion fabric while the project is still in pieces in order to give more body and durability to the finished piece. In this case, I bonded the heavy-duty interfacing to muslin and flat lined those both to the fashion fabric so that when the handbag is handled the fashion fabric and interfacing aren't bonded directly and don't end up with permanent wrinkles after being turned. This gives the finished bag a more refined look than if the interfacing were bonded directly to the fabric. Follow the steps below to flat line:

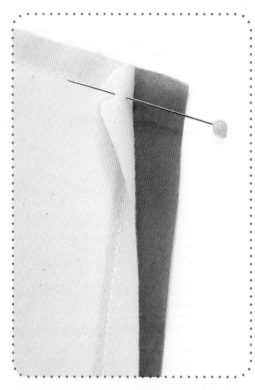

Flat line the bag pieces with the pre-interfaced muslin. This sandwiches the heavy-duty interfacing between your outer fabric and your muslin.

1 Apply heavy-duty interfacing to the flat-lining fabric. Make sure to cut the seam allowances away on the interfacing so the seam allowance is just one layer of fabric. This is different from the lightweight interfacing we have used in previous chapters. With lightweight interfacing you can leave the seam allowances on and it won't make a difference in the sewing.

2 Take all muslin flat-lining pieces with interfacing attached and apply them to the bag pieces with wrong sides together. Stitch all around the edges with a machine-basting stitch just inside the seam allowance line so that when the handbag is sewn together you won't see these stitches. They are basted because if they do show in the finished project they can be easily removed.

As in the other chapters, assemble the smaller components first and then sew those pieces together. With this in mind, construct the handles first by folding the outer edges of the handle sections over, secure them with pins or tape, and topstitch. This project may call for experimenting with scraps and some sample passes, as well as with different stitch lengths and widths with the topstitching distance from the edge. In fact, for each of the examples in this book that include topstitching, I took a moment before stitching and made a sample in order to have the most pleasing stitch length and proportion for the width of a topstitched edge.

1 Create pleating on the handbag front piece by stitching down piece C in the middle, then pinning both B pieces with right sides together on either side, and stitch. Press open toward the outer edges of the bag if this is a fabric you can press. (I left these sections unpressed to make the piecing look more like pleats than pieced sections.) Then put the A pieces on either end, again making sure to keep the right sides together. Stitch, press if needed, and then stitch the outer edges down so that you now have one complete front piece.

2 Flat line the front and back pieces to the interfaced muslin pieces (see page 145), making sure to stitch them together outside of the final seam line.

3 Assemble the outside of the handbag by stitching the right sides of the bag and its sides together. Leave the bottom open.

4 Align the long sides of the bottom piece to the corresponding long side of the back piece and stitch this line. Then pin both of the side bottom seams, clipping into the corner of the front/bottom piece so that the stitching lines can be matched evenly across. Stitch the bottom of the bag at the sides to create the flat bottom.

5 Assemble the lining as the outer bag was assembled, but leave the bottom seam open for turning.

6 Stitch the handles onto the bag. Pin first and check the angle so that the handles will end up where they are sewn. Make any adjustments in

A Attach the handles to the bag prior to attaching the lining so they'll be sewn into the top edge seam when the lining and bag are sewn together.

the angle, repin, and then stitch. Temporarily pin the handles to the inside of the bag so that they aren't loose and won't get caught in the seam allowance when you're adding the lining (see **A**).

7 Turn the lining inside out and put the outer bag inside it. Pin along the top edge with right sides together and stitch all around (see **B**).

8 Trim around the sewn edge, clipping into curves and grading seams as you go to make the turned edge less bulky.

9 Turn the bag right side out with the lining now on the inside of the bag. Press the top edge of the bag from the inside (see **C**).

10 Pin the bottom seam, pulling it out of the bag enough to stitch the seam by hand with an invisible blindstitch (see **D**).

11 Apply the fastening hardware according to the manufacturer's directions. For this metal frame with the kiss clasp, you apply glue to the top edge of the bag and to the inside of the metal frame. Allow the adhesive to dry for about fifteen minutes or until dry to the touch.

12 Very carefully join the bag and the frame, being sure to center the bag

B The assembled bag exterior turned inside out with handles attached, ready to receive the lining.

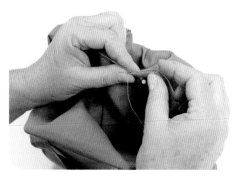

D Stitching the lining closed while pulled up and through the opening of the bag.

C

The finished handbag.

page 150   page 152   page 154   page 156   page 160

Above are some of the possible variations you can achieve with the source handbag pattern.

HANDBAG VARIATIONS

The following variations on our source handbag show the wide spectrum of results you can get from a single rub-off pattern. Once you master the patterning technique, you'll quickly realize that you have a potentially unlimited pattern supply all around you. This pattern is broken down to its most basic form and reduced in size in a simple clutch pattern. Variations of fabric and handle choice show what a difference color and texture can make. Larger, yet still classic shapes, such as a casual cotton tote and a bowling bag–style yoga bag, give examples of what can be achieved by manipulating the size and shape of the source handbag pattern. From the metal frame with a kiss clasp to magnetic closures and even a zipper, this source handbag shape lends itself to just about any closure you can find to create an entire wardrobe of bags.

Bamboo Handbag

This handbag is taken from our source handbag pattern using a softer, mint cotton fabric and bamboo handles. The great thing about these simple shapes is that a change of fabric can transform the entire mood of the piece. Instead of the fabric handles from our source, a purchased set of bamboo handles was used. The handles are attached with matching rick rack by looping the rick rack around the bamboo handles and then attaching them the same as you would the fabric handles. The structured metal hardware closure of the source bag is substituted with a clean finished open top with easy-to-install magnetic closures.

PREPARING THE LINING AND APPLYING THE RICK RACK STRIPS

1 Prepare the lining for closures by reinforcing the top edge of each piece with a narrow strip of the exterior fabric.

2 Cut four strips of 2 inch- wide fabric and press under ¼ inch on each edge. (You could use strips of fabric instead of rick rack, if you'd like.) Apply the strips to the top of the lining piece by topstitching (see **A**).

3 Flat line and assemble (see page 145) all the pieces.

4 Secure the bamboo loops to the rick rack strips. Attach the rick rack strips at the same place we did for the source handbag handles (see **B**).

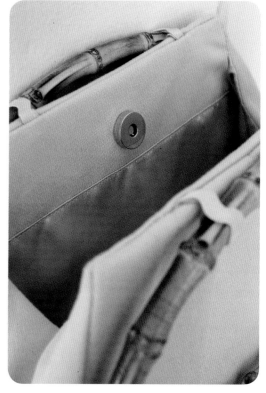

A Rick rack strips secure the bamboo handles. Strips of outer fabric reinforce the closure area of the lining.

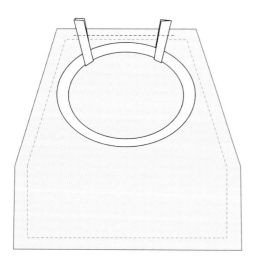

B Topstitching the rick rack strips to the top of the lining.

This handbag variation uses the same pattern derived from the source bag, but substitutes bamboo handles.

5 O'Clock Handbag

This clever Amy Butler fabric is called Tangerine Martini. It gives a festive touch to our original source handbag. The sides are made of a coordinating silk I repurposed from a damaged vintage kimono. The metal handbag frame was purchased from a craft store and applied to the top edge of the bag with jewelry adhesive.

APPLYING THE HANDLES AND LINING

1 Apply the ribbon handles flat, before sewing the bag (see **A**).

2 Catch the ribbon ends in the bottom seam when sewing the exterior.

3 Apply the lining the same way as the source handbag (see pages 146–147). Be sure to pin the ribbon handles out of the way when attaching the lining.

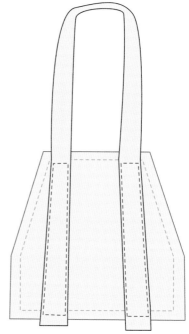

A Sew the ribbon handles onto the pieces while they're flat and catch the ends in the bottom seam.

Jewelry adhesive binds the metal frame.

This variation is a flirty, casual take on the original source handbag. It shows how you can achieve an entirely different look by simply changing the fabric and letting the print speak for itself.

Ladylike Tote

In this variation, the source handbag pattern was blown up to triple its original size to create this practical tote bag. The lining is a coordinating heavy home decor–weight cotton fabric, and the straps are sturdy cotton webbing, which were applied to the front and back pieces while they were flat. The ends were caught in the bottom seam when it was sewn, similar to the ribbon handles in the 5 O'clock handbag on page 152. The shape of the side gussets in this larger variation makes it a bit more refined than the classic canvas tote, and the angle of the handles adds further interest.

1 Take the source bag pattern and trace it onto another sheet of kraft paper using a needle wheel.

2 Draw two crossing lines to divide each piece in half both horizontally and vertically.

3 Cut out the pattern pieces apart along the lines and spread them until you have your desired size (see **A**).

4 Tape the spread pieces to another sheet of kraft paper and connect the outer edges with lines, making the new outline of the larger pattern piece.

5 Do the same with every other piece, making sure that every line which will be joined is the same length. Adjusting the bottom of the bag will make the entire tote much wider at the bottom, so you'll need to match the width of the side gusset to the width of the side of the bottom where they will join when sewing.

6 Pinch in and tack the side gussets with hand-stitched pleats to maintain the shape of the tote (see **B**).

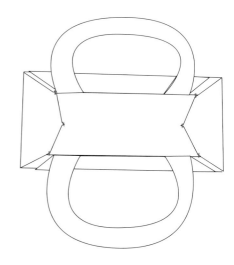

B Control the shape of the sides by pinching and tacking the corners in the direction you'd like them to go.

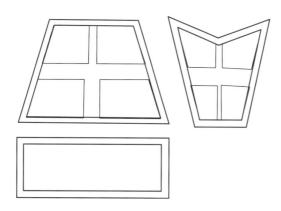

A The source handbag pattern is blown up for the tote.

C The lining.

This sturdy variation is a fresh take on the classic canvas tote.

Yoga Bag

Our tote pattern is taken one step further by rounding the edges to accommodate a heavy-duty zipper. A strap for carrying a mat or jacket was added by inserting black grosgrain ribbon loops in the bottom seam of the bag and then threading thick cord elastic through the loops. The strap hides along the bottom when not in use.

CONVERTING THE SOURCE HANDBAG

1 Trace the source handbag pattern onto another piece of kraft paper and mark perpendicular cross points in the center of all the pattern pieces.

2 Cut the pieces apart and pin them to the paper marked with perpendicular lines, expanding the pattern until you get the desired size.

3 When you achieve the size and proportion you want, tape the pieces down and redraw your exterior lines.

4 If you're making the bag deeper as well as larger, slash and spread the side pieces as well.

5 Now slash and spread the bottom and add the amount to each axis that corresponds to the desired width and depth of the new bag.

6 This is where you can add pockets to either the inside, outside, or both. I rounded the corners of the bag to accommodate a double zipper along the top edge. Once you have the pattern enlarged to the desired size and style, add the seam allowances with your pencil and clear gridded ruler.

7 Make sure all pieces are labeled with name, grain line, seam allowance, cutting instructions, sewing instructions, gathers, etc.

8 Cut the new bag and mark all necessary notches or dots.

9 As in other projects, sew the component parts like the handles first, making sure to make a sample for the topstitching.

The interior, with a contrasting lining zipper opening.

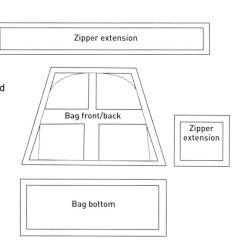

Ⓐ The source bag pattern is expanded and rounded to create this bowling bag shape.

A heavy-duty zipper and ribbon loops make this tote perfect for carrying just about anything you may need for a day's outing.

APPLYING THE ZIPPER

1 Assemble any zippered areas, as these are more difficult to do when the bag is further along.

2 Using a zipper foot on your sewing machine, apply the extension or flange piece on one side of the zipper and the lining piece behind the zipper. Fold both the front and lining flanges away from the teeth of the zipper and topstitch the fabric down so that it won't interfere with the action of the zipper opening and closing. Topstitch ¼ inch from the edge. Repeat with both the outer fabric and lining on the other side of the zipper. You should now have a rectangular piece with a zipper down the middle that has the outer bag fabric on one side and the lining fabric on the back side that's topstitched ¼ inch away from the zipper edge on both sides (see **A**).

3 Stitch the extension pieces across the top and bottom areas of the zipper. Then do the same to the lining pieces. Turn and topstitch ¼ inch from the edge as in the side extension pieces (see **B**). You now should have a framed zipper and an assembled section that's ready to join with the front, back, and bottom.

4 Interface and flat line the bag as needed for your fabric choice.

5 Apply the handles as in the previous handbag projects.

6 Pin the zipper section between both side sections and sew.

7 Attach ribbon loops to the edges of the bag bottom so that just enough of the loop will be exposed when the bag is sewn together for the elastic cording to be threaded through.

8 Pin the bottom of the bag to the rest of the bag and then sew around each side, making sure to sew the one stitch across the corner point as in the sewing corners section (see page 25).

9 Grade the seam allowances and trim across the corners.

10 Repeat with the remaining lining pieces.

11 Turn the bag inside out and the lining right side out. Pin the lining to the bag's interior and hand-stitch the lining to the bag to create a tidy interior.

12 Flip the bag right side out and thread the elastic cording through the ribbon loops. Thread the elastic through a purchased cord stopper made for this purpose and available in the notions department of fabric stores.

Leather and vinyl need a little extra care when sewing.

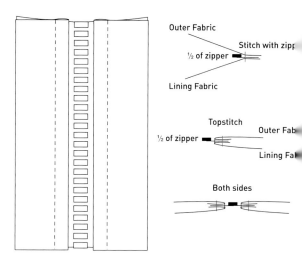

Outer Fabric
Stitch with zipp
½ of zipper
Lining Fabric

Topstitch
Outer Fab
½ of zipper
Lining Fa

Both sides

A Applying flange and lining piece to each side of the zipper, fold, and topstitch.

Folded Out

Folded

B Applying extension pieces to both ends of the zipper, turn, and topstitch.

Use the following tips when working with them:

1 Lay out the pieces and mark around them with a pen or Sharpie.

2 Cut the pieces with either scissors or a rotary cutter.

3 When sewing, use clips instead of pins.

4 Use a leather or denim needle in your sewing machine (leather needles have a knife edge).

5 Make a stitching sample on a scrap before you sew the real piece.

6 Use a heavier thread than you would use for fabric sewing. Button, upholstery, or craft thread are some of the heavier weights available.

7 To keep the pieces feeding smoothly, use a walking foot or a Teflon foot, or slip tissue paper between the foot and the leather.

A clever trick I learned from my super-crafty fellow patternmaker Ellen Allen is to use baby powder applied with a blush brush as you sew. This works especially well on extra glossy vinyl.

Fur Clutch

By shortening one side of the source handbag and narrowing the bottom, you can make an elegant clutch. The simplicity of the shape is a perfect match for this sleek faux fur. The sides are kept streamlined by substituting with black wool, which maintains the color but gives it a tailored feel.

1 Trace the source bag pattern piece that includes the bottom of the bag onto another sheet of kraft paper.

2 Cut out the new back and bottom piece so that you can fold it to the size you would like your clutch to be.

3 Play with the size and shape by folding the bottom up and making the top edge fold down like an envelope. This will distort where the bottom is, but don't worry about it now.

4 Make a fold line that will accommodate the thickness of the faux fur where the flap of the envelope folds over so that it will lie down nicely. The extra fold area that will extend from the back of the bag to the flap should be about ¼ inch wide to fold comfortably.

5 Now turn the folded piece over and notice that the edges of the front side extend past the edges of the back side. Draw in the shape of the back with pencil, unfold, and trim the extra bits from either side.

6 Refold the bag pattern into the envelope shape and look at it from the side. Open up the fold and create the new bottom by allowing about 1½ inches to sit as the new bottom, making sure that both the front and back are even so the clutch will be balanced if you sit it on a flat surface.

7 Unfold the paper again and true up (see page 34) the edges of the new bottom by drawing straight lines between the two ends of the folded lines.

8 Look at the pattern and decide which areas will be fur and which will be lining. Make a line of notation on the pattern and then trace each individual section onto another sheet of kraft paper to make those other component pattern pieces.

9 Measure the depth of the bottom of the bag and draw a line that's the same length on another sheet of kraft paper to begin the pattern for the side gusset.

A magnetic snap closure.

Shortening a side and narrowing the
bottom converts our source handbag
pattern into an elegant-looking clutch.

10 Measure the height of the front and back areas to get the height of the side gusset. Make two lines this distance up from each end of the bottom line of the new gusset piece. If this is as much as you would like the bag to open, then you have your pattern piece. If you would like it to open a bit wider, then pivot these lines out to make a wider top edge of the gusset piece. Just be sure that the length of the sides of the pattern piece remains the same as you pivot so that it will fit into the shape of the clutch (see **A**).

11 When you're happy with the width of the top of the gusset, you can either leave it straight across the top or taper it down toward the middle, as in the source gusset pattern. Either method simply removes a bit of bulk from the interior by tapering it.

12 To make the clutch, cut out all the pieces from the fur that you'd like to reinforce. Then cut the lining, muslin, and interfacing. When cutting the lining, make sure to cut it in two pieces so there can be a seam at the bottom of the inside of the bag to flip the bag right side out after sewing. Note that I have made the gussets in this clutch out of a coordinating black wool-cashmere coating fabric. It's still sturdy but not as thick as the faux fur.

13 Bond interfacing to the tracing fabric for flat lining. Make sure you don't put interfacing in the ¼- inch-wide section that acts as the "hinge" area for your flap. This will ensure that your bag closes nicely.

14 Flat line the interfaced tracing fabric piece to the fur piece.

15 Stitch the side gussets to the back of the bag, then the front, and then across the bottom edges, clipping into the corners in order to make the seam allowances match more easily.

16 Repeat with the lining, making sure to keep an opening in the bottom so that you can turn the bag through it after you join the lining and outer bag.

17 Before attaching the lining, apply the magnetic closure as seen in the Bamboo Handbag (see page 150). Make sure you think through where the closure will go when the bag is assembled—once you make the holes for the prongs, you're stuck with them (see **B**).

18 After you've finished the magnetic closure, keep the bag inside out and apply the lining by stitching all around the upper edge.

19 Clip into the curves and then trim and grade the seams. Then, flip the entire arrangement through the opening at the bottom of the lining.

Leave this area without interfacing to create a soft hinge for the flap

Flap

Back

Equal Lengths

Side

Bottom

Equal Lengths

Front

A Shortening one side to create a clutch pattern.

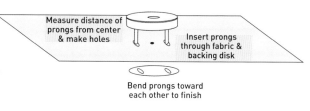

Measure distance of prongs from center & make holes

Insert prongs through fabric & backing disk

Bend prongs toward each other to finish

B Applying the magnetic closure.

20 Because of the small area you're working with, you'll need to finish the top edge and any other areas you'd like to topstitch with a handworked **pick stitch**. This adds to the overall tailored quality of the bag.

21 I arranged the gussets to the inside of the bag and pick stitched the seam to make sure they stay in. Tuck in any stray shaping of the fur with hand-stitching, and the bag is complete!

Black wool sides give the clutch a tailored look.

WORKING WITH HEAVY FABRIC AND FAKE FUR

A bulky fabric like fake Persian lamb will translate nicely in the flatter areas of the bag, but will be bulky in the tighter areas, so choose a complementary fabric to work in its place. In our clutch variation, I used the fur only on the major focal areas and a lighter, more malleable weight of fabric on the sides. This makes for a more elegantly proportioned bag. You can also use a leather or vinyl on the bottom of the bag to make it more durable. When working with fake fur, follow these guidelines. They also apply to real fur, which I prefer not to use:

1 Make a note of the nap direction on the wrong side of the fabric. Mark with an arrow using a Sharpie or other appropriate marker.

2 Place your pieces and mark on the wrong side of the fabric.

3 Cut carefully with blunt-tip scissors through the fabric, making sure not to cut the fur. This may seem unnecessary on shorter furs, but when working with longer furs it's very important. You want to maintain the length all the way to the seam allowance or you'll end up with weird chunks missing, which is not pretty.

4 After you sew the seams together, you can then use a comb to gently remove the fur that's caught in the seam allowance and blend the fur so that the seam disappears.

RESOURCES

FABRIC

Amy Butler
www.amybutlerdesign.com

Oilcloth International
www.oilcloth.com

The Fabric Fairy
www.thefabricfairy.com

Vogue Fabrics
www.voguefabrics.com

Gayfeather Fabrics
www.gayfeatherfabrics.com

Stitcher's Crossing
www.stitcherscrossing.com

Mill House Quilts
www.millhousequilts.com

JoAnn Fabrics
www.joann.com

TOOLS & FINDINGS

Fiskars
www.fiskars.com

Nancy's Notions
www.nancysnotions.com

Acme Notions
www.acmenotions.com

B. Black & Sons Tailoring Supply
www.bblackandsons.com

Joggles
www.joggles.com

Richard the Thread
www.richardthethread.com

Finebrand
www.finebrand.com

Stitchcoach
www.stitchcoach.com

VINTAGE CLOTHING

Lou Rags
www.luvvintage.com

Ragstock
www.ragstock.com

FURTHER INSTRUCTION

Stitchcoach
www.stitchcoach.com

GLOSSARY

A

angle
Plastic 45-degree triangle used to find and mark 90-degree angles for perpendicular lines.

assemble
To put together or build.

awl
A hand tool with a very sharp pointed tip used primarily to make holes. It can also be used to help push fabric along when machine-sewing something that can't be held with the fingers.

B

backstitch
To reverse direction and sew an extra stitch, then traveling forward again from the underside of the fabric.

baste
To sew loosely with a large running stitch. Used to temporarily secure pieces together or mark something.

bias
The direction of fabric that's on a diagonal angle from the running length of the fabric. "True bias" is exactly 45 degrees from the straight of grain.

blindstitch
To carefully sew so the stitches aren't visible from the outside of the work.

bustline
The line running parallel to the ground that's at the fullest part of the chest over the bust and around the back.

C

center back
The center line of the body as seen from the back. The line that divides the back of the body down the middle. Abbreviated as CB.

center front
The center line of the body as seen from the front. The line that divides the front of the body down the middle. Abbreviated as CF.

chevron
A V-shape created when two pieces of fabric with a linear pattern come together at an angle. If these lines are matched properly at the seam line we say that it "chevrons."

cross grain
The direction of fabric that's perpendicular to the running length of the fabric.

curve tools
Measuring tools used to create smooth curved lines. Sometimes called a "design ruler" or "dressmaker's curve," some feature combined curves used in an armhole and neckline; others are "hip curves," which are a composite of a typical shape of the curve of a hip, used in patterning skirts and pants.

D

dart
A triangular-shaped wedge that's drawn on a pattern and marked and sewn into a garment in order to make the flat piece curve around the body.

draping

The process of creating a garment or a pattern by placing fabric over an object, smoothing and clipping the fabric, and pinning together the necessary pieces as you go.

E

ease

The amount of fabric that's in addition to the exact measurement of the figure being fit. Also the process of making two pieces of fabric with slightly different measurements fit together smoothly.

F

facing

A piece of fabric that's meant to conceal and enclose the raw edge of an opening, such as a neckline or an armhole.

fold line

The folded edge of a piece of fabric that's laid out for cutting a garment.

French cuffs

A style of sleeve cuff that's twice as long as a standard cuff and meant to be folded in half and fastened with cuff links; most often seen in men's dress shirts.

French curve

A curved ruler with multiple curved edges, and used in patternmaking to smooth the smaller curves of a pocket, cuff, or collar pattern.

G

gather

To compress fabric into a smaller amount of space by making a running stitch and then pulling the thread so that the fabric forms into multiple mounds on either side of the stitching line.

grading

Grading a seam is to trim one side of the fabric slightly smaller than the other in order to reduce the bulk at the edge. This creates a smoother, more finished garment.

gridded ruler

A clear plastic ruler that has a grid printed on it. It's used to measure, draw in straight lines, and to draw in seam allowances by placing the grid lines on the finished edge of the pattern piece and making consistent markings around the periphery of the finished lines, creating a consistent seam allowance without having to separately measure the seam allowance and then go back and connect the lines later.

H

hem

To create a finished edge on the bottom of a garment or sleeve. Also the area that has been hemmed.

Hug-Snug

A brand of rayon seam binding that's available through tailor supply shops.

I

interfacing

A layer of fabric, found in varying thicknesses and stiffness, depending on the application, which is applied to the inside of a piece of fabric to stabilize or otherwise make it more substantial or less transparent. Available in sew-in or fusible types.

invisible marker
A marker with ink that disappears either after time or when wet. These must be used carefully as the ink can tend to "ghost" back into view under certain lighting or if the ink is heated before it's removed.

K
knitted fabric
A type of fabric formed by looping fibers together in a knitting process. Distinguishable from a "woven" by the appearance of the fibers looped together as opposed to a grid of fibers found in a woven fabric.

kraft paper
Brown paper used in making patterns, usually found in the shipping supplies section of office supply and other retail stores.

M
machine-baste
To make a loose basting stitch using the sewing machine, typically at the highest stitch length setting available.

miter
To make a seam at a diagonal angle, joining two hems that intersect at a corner.

muslin
An inexpensive cotton woven fabric that's often used in draping patterns and to make "mock-up" garments used for fitting accuracy.

N
nap
The piled surface of a fabric.

needle wheel
A tool similar to a tracing wheel but with very sharp points that are able to puncture paper.

notches
Small areas clipped into the seam allowance of a pattern to indicate information about the piece, such as location on the garment and junctures with other pieces.

O
overlock
A type of stitch that finishes off the edges of a cut piece of fabric. A machine that makes this stitch and trims the edge of the fabric (also called a serger or marrow machine).

P
pattern notcher
A tool similar to a hole punch used to make notches on paper pattern pieces. Found at patternmaking and tailor supply vendors.

pick stitch
A very small decorative backstitch used in place of topstitching to secure an outer layer of fabric; often found in tailored clothing.

placket
A type of finishing for any sort of opening where a continuous strip of fabric is stitched to the raw edge and then folded and stitched to bind off the raw edge. Seen often on shirt sleeves.

pleats
A fold of fabric that adds fullness into a garment.

point turner
A handheld tool used to push out the point of an area that has been stitched and then turned, as in the point of a collar.

press on
A term that's often used interchangeably with fusible; common term for fusible interfacing, "press-on" interfacing or just "press-on."

press open
To open a seam that has been stitched using an iron.

pressing area
Ironing board or dedicated table in a sewing workroom equipped with an iron and all other pressing equipment.

pressing cloth
A piece of fabric that's placed over the work so that the iron doesn't touch it directly, keeping steam and heat from overly flattening the surface of the fabric or make it shiny.

pressing ham
A stuffed, rounded pressing tool used to press curved shapes.

R

roll hem
A very tiny hem worked by machine or hand, often seen on the edge of delicate fabrics. The fabric is "rolled" over so that the raw edge is covered with fabric and then the edge is secured with a delicate row of topstitching. Common on scarves and sheer skirts.

ruching
Another term for gathers. To condense fabric into a smaller surface area by pulling a running stitch that has been made across its surface.

running stitch
A straight stitch, often larger than a standard garment sewing stitch.

S

S
Abbreviation for "side."

SB
Abbreviation for "side back."

seam allowance
The area between the raw edge of fabric and the stitch that holds two pieces together.

seam ripper
A pointed, handheld tool that allows you to pick out stitches that you would like to remove, or cut many stitched continuously by running the sharp edge along the seam.

selvage
The edge of a piece of fabric, usually denser and less flexible than the rest, made as the result of the manufacturing process. These areas have more shrinkage usually and should be clipped intermittently when a fabric has been prewashed so that the fabric spreads evenly across the cutting area.

side back
A pattern or garment piece that attaches to the side seam on one side and to the back piece on the other side. Abbreviated as SB.

side front
A pattern or garment piece that attaches to the side seam on one side and to the front piece on the other side. Abbreviated as SF.

silk pins
Very thin, sharp type of straight pins ideal for use in fine, delicate, or very dense fabrics.

sleeve board
A small ironing surface that's about 4 inches wide, used to press open sleeves, pant legs, or other areas that cannot be laid out on a flat surface.

staystitching
A row of stitching used to stabilize an area that's likely to stretch out during the handling process, such as a neckline or armhole. Can be used anywhere stability is needed.

straight of grain
The direction that runs the length of the piece of fabric, parallel to the selvage edge.

T

tailor's chalk
A chalky or waxy marking tool that's easily removed after the garment is sewn.

tailor's board
A wooden pressing tool that has multiple pressing surfaces for pressing points and small curves.

thread baste
To loosely sew something together temporarily for sewing or pressing instead of using pins.

topstitching
A row of stitching that usually runs parallel to the edge of a garment.

tracing paper
A type of paper covered in a waxy or chalky film, used with a tracing wheel to mark fabric.

tracing wheel
A handheld tool used in conjunction with colored tracing paper. The teeth on the wheel pick up color from the surface of tracing paper and transfer it to the fabric.

twill tape
A woven ribbon that's distinguished by its twill weave pattern. Usually cotton, in black or white, and available in multiple widths.

W

warp
In a woven fabric, the fibers that run the length of the fabric.

weft
In a woven fabric, the fibers that run perpendicular to the selvage edge.

welt
The covered edge of an opening used to bind and conceal the raw fabric edge when a slit's needed from the exterior to the interior of a garment. Used for pockets and bound buttonholes.

woven
Fabric that's manufactured by "weaving" fibers together using a loom. Distinguished by the crosshatching pattern created when fibers are joined at right angles.

Y

yardstick
A measuring tool, usually wooden, that's 36 inches long.

Z

zigzag
A stitch that goes from right to left, creating small points on either side.

INDEX

A

Aligning stripes, 56
A-Line Money Dress, 90–91
Altering patterns, 38–39
Angle-measuring tools, 16

B

Blouse pattern variations, 125–137
    about: summary of, 125
    Cap Sleeve Summer Sky Blouse, 130–131
    Green Apple Blouse with Cuffs, 126–127
    Little Black Blouse with Darts, 128–129
    Rock-a-Billy Blouse, 132–133
    Shanti Tunic, 134–137
Blouses, patterning, 102–125
    adding measurements, 108
    adding seam allowances, 112
    advanced slashing and spreading, 111
    altering pattern, 110–111
    creating facings, 112
    creating pattern, 110–112
    cutting fabric, 113
    finished blouse, 124
    hemming and applying buttons, 122–123
    sewing. See Sewing blouse pieces
    source blouse for, 102–103
    tracing source blouse, 104–108
    variations. See Blouse pattern variations
Buttonhole placement, 121
Buttons, applying, 123

C

Cap Sleeve Summer Sky Blouse, 130–131
Ceiling-tile-covered table, 20
Concave curves, sewing, 24
Convex curves, sewing, 25
Corners, sewing, 25
Cotton Bias-Cut Skirt, 60–63
Cross grain, 20
Cuff links, making, 123, 128
Curves
    concave, sewing, 24
    convex, sewing, 24
    measuring tools, 16
Cutting fabric
    blouse patterns, 113
    dress patterns, 74

handbag pattern, 144
quickly without pins, 74
skirt patterns, 40–41
tools for, 17, 41

D

Darts
    adding/adjusting measurements, 34
    alternate methods for making, 113
    stitching, for dress, 75
    stitching, for skirt, 42
Casual Denim Skirt, 48, 49
Do-Sew™, 17
Dress pattern variations, 85–99
    about: summary of, 85
    A-Line Money Dress, 90–91
    Inner Audrey Princess Seam Dress, 92–93
    Pin-Up Halter Dress, 96–99
    Retro V-Neck Dress, 86–89
    Vintage Shop 'Til You Drop Dress, 94–95
Dresses, patterning (fabric rub-off method), 66–85
    about: overview of method, 15, 67
    adding seam allowances, 73
    altering pattern, 71–72
    creating dress and facing patterns, 71–73
    cutting fabric, 74
    finished dress, 84
    hemming dress, 84
    sewing. See Sewing dress pieces
    source dress for, 66
    tracing source dress, 68–70
    variations. See Dress pattern variations

E

Easestitching, 75, 76
Estimating yardage, 22

F

Fabric
    aligning stripes/patterns, 56
    cutting, 40–41
    estimating yardage, 22
    grain lines, 20
    heavy, sewing, 163
    knits vs. wovens, 20
Fabric rub-off method
    overview of, 15, 67

steps. *See Dresses, patterning (fabric rub-off method)*
Facings and interfacings, 18, 45, 72, 81–82, 112, 120. *See also specific patterns*
Flat lining, 145
French curve, 16
Fur, sewing, 163

G
Glossary, 166–170
Grain lines, 20
Green Apple Blouse with Cuffs, 126–127

H
Handbag pattern variations, 149–163
    about: summary of, 149; sewing leather and vinyl, 159
    Bamboo Handbag, 150–151
    5 O'clock Handbag, 152–153
    Fur clutch, 160–163
    Ladylike Tote, 154–155
    Yoga Bag, 156–159
Handbags, patterning, 140–149
    creating pattern, 143
    cutting fabric, 144
    learning about handles, 143
    sewing bag, 146–148
    source handbag, 140–141
    tracing handbag, 142
    variations. *See Handbag pattern variations*
Hemming
    blouse, 122–123
    dress, 84
    skirt, 46

I
Inner Audrey Princess Seam Dress, 92–93
Inner structure/finish items, 18
Interfacings. *See Facings and interfacings*
Iron and pressing tools, 18

K
Kick pleat, adding, 50
Knitted fabric, 20
Kraft paper, for paper rub-off, 14

L
Labeling pattern pieces, 36
Leather, sewing, 159
Little Black Blouse with Darts, 128–129

M
Marking tools, 16
Measurements
    adding/adjusting dart/pleat measurements, 34, 108
    taking, 23
Measuring tools, 16

N
Needle wheels, 15, 16, 38
Notching, 37, 113

O
Overlocking, 77

P
Paper rub-off method
    ceiling-tile-covered table for, 20
    overview of, 14, 29
    steps. *See Skirts, patterning (paper rub-off method)*
Pattern notcher, 16
Pattern weights, 17
Patterning supplies, 17
Patterns (within fabric), matching, 56
Pinking after sewing, 77
Pins
    choosing, 19
    cutting quickly without, 74
Pin-Up Halter Dress, 96–99
Pockets, in skirts, 49, 60–63
Pressing tools, 18
Princess seam dress, 92–93

R
Resources, 164
Retro V-Neck Dress, 86–89
Reversible Cotton Wrap Skirt, 57–59
Rock-a-Billy Blouse, 132–133
Rotary cutters, 17, 41
Rub-off technique
    fabric. *See Fabric rub-off method*
    paper. *See Paper rub-off method*
    reasons to learn, 11

S
Seam allowances, adding, 39, 73, 112
Sewing
    concave curves, 24
    convex curves, 25
    corners, 25
    fur, 163
    heavy fabric, 163
    leather, 159
    skirt pattern, 42–44
    tools for, 18
    vinyl, 159
Sewing blouse pieces, 114–121
    buttonhole placement, 121
    collar trick, 114
    cuffs, 115, 118–119
    facings and upper collar, 120
    pleats and darts, 115
    shoulder seams, 116
    side seams, 116
    sleeves, 117
Sewing dress pieces, 75–83
    assembling/connecting back and front, 78–79
    darts, 75
    easestitching, 75, 76
    facings, 81–82
    inserting zipper, 42–44
    order of, 83
    pinking or overlocking after, 77
    pressing and, 75
    quick fitting and, 80
    setting in sleeves, 80–81
    staystitching, 75, 76
Sewing handbag, 146–148
Shanti Tunic, 134–137
Shark, making, 126
Shears and cutters, 17, 41
Skirt pattern variations, 47–63
    about: summary of, 47
    Casual Denim Skirt, 48, 49
    Cotton Bias-Cut Skirt, 60–63
    Reversible Cotton Wrap Skirt, 57–59
    Striped A-Line Skirt, 54–56
    Wool Tweed City Skirt, 50–51
Skirts, patterning (paper rub-off method), 28–47
    about: overview of method, 14, 29
    adding seam allowances, 39

adding/adjusting dart measurements, 34
altering pattern, 38–39
altering vintage garments for modern fit, 35
applying waistband, 45
creating paper pattern, 33–39
cutting fabric, 40–41
finished skirt, 46
fitting skirt, 44
hemming skirt, 46
inserting zipper, 42–44, 52–53
labeling pattern pieces, 36
notching, 37
sewing skirt, 42–44
source skirt for, 28
stitching darts, 42
tracing source skirt, 30–32
variations. *See Skirt pattern variations*
Source items
    blouse, 102–103
    dress, 66
    handbag, 140–141
    skirt, 28
Staystitching, 75, 76
Straight of grain, 20
Striped A-Line Skirt, 54–56
Stripes, aligning, 56
Supplies. *See Tools and equipment*

T
Tailor's chalk, 16
Tape, bias and twill, 18
Tape and dispenser, 17
Tools and equipment, 16–19
    choosing right pins, 19
    cutting tools, 17
    inner structure/finish items, 18
    marking tools, 16
    measuring tools, 16
    patterning supplies, 17
    pressing tools, 18
    sewing tools, 18
Topstitching, 122–123
Tracing source items
    blouse, 104–108
    dress, 68–70
    handbag, 142
    skirt, 30–32

Tracing wheels, 16, 41
Twill tape, 18

V
Vintage garments, altering for modern fit, 35
Vintage Shop 'Til You Drop Dress, 94–95
Vinyl, sewing, 159

W
Waistband
    applying, 45
    patterning, 32
    tracing, 32
Wool Tweed City Skirt, 50–51
Woven fabric, 20

Y
Yardage, estimating, 22

Z
Zippers
    applying to handbag, 158
    basting, 43
    hand finishing for couture look, 52–53
    inserting in dress, 78
    inserting in skirt, 42–44

METRIC CONVERSION CHART

TO CONVERT	TO	MULTIPLY BY
Inches	Centimeters	2.54
Centimeters	Inches	0.4
Feet	Centimeters	30.5
Centimeters	Feet	0.03
Yards	Meters	0.9
Meters	Yards	1.1
Sq. Inches	Sq. Centimeters	5.45
Sq. Centimeters	Sq. Inches	0.16
Sq. Feet	Sq. Meters	0.09
Sq. Meters	Sq. Feet	10.8
Sq. Yards	Sq. Meters	0.8
Sq. Meters	Sq. Yards	1.2